Mr. Teel spent 18 years teaching elementary school, primarily in a self-contained setting. He recently moved to Boerne, Texas to be closer to his sons and grandson. He spends his time trying to stay in shape, tutoring, and writing children's stories. He is working on a follow-up to *Richard,* tentatively titled, *Sweet Tea and a Ding Dong.*

I would like to thank all of my students, their parents, my co-workers, my principals, and those special teachers of mine who worked so hard to build meaningful relationships over the years. And for believing in the Power of a Triangle.

And for my own family at home. Love you.

Stephen Teel

WHO IS RICHARD STANDS AND WHY DO OUR CHILDREN PLEDGE THEIR ALLEGIANCE TO HIM?

AUSTIN MACAULEY PUBLISHERS™
LONDON • CAMBRIDGE • NEW YORK • SHARJAH

Copyright © Stephen Teel 2024

All rights reserved. No part of this publication may be reproduced, distributed, or transmitted in any form or by any means, including photocopying, recording, or other electronic or mechanical methods, without the prior written permission of the publisher, except in the case of brief quotations embodied in critical reviews and certain other non-commercial uses permitted by copyright law. For permission requests, write to the publisher.

Any person who commits any unauthorized act in relation to this publication may be liable to criminal prosecution and civil claims for damages.

All of the events in this memoir are true to the best of author's memory. The views expressed in this memoir are solely those of the author.

Ordering Information
Quantity sales: Special discounts are available on quantity purchases by corporations, associations, and others. For details, contact the publisher at the address below.

Publisher's Cataloging-in-Publication data
Teel, Stephen
Who is Richard Stands and Why Do Our Children Pledge Their Allegiance to Him?

ISBN 9781649794499 (Paperback)
ISBN 9781638290810 (Hardback)
ISBN 9781638290865 (ePub e-book)
ISBN 9781649794512 (Audiobook)

Library of Congress Control Number: 2023905072

www.austinmacauley.com/us

First Published 2024
Austin Macauley Publishers LLC
40 Wall Street 33rd Floor, Suite 3302
New York, NY 10005
USA

mail-usa@austinmacauley.com
+1 (646) 5125767

Without the encouragement and support of Carolyn, this book would still be in my head.

Table of Contents

Introduction	**11**
Part One: The What	**13**
Chapter One: Every Teacher Has One. Here's Mine	*15*
Chapter Two: Beginnings	*17*
Chapter Three: The Power of a Triangle	*20*
Chapter Four: How to Get Parents on Board and How to Have a Successful Year Even If They Don't	*23*
Chapter Five: Parent/Teacher Conferences. Be the Expert in the Room.	*26*
Chapter Six: I Love That Kid!	*31*
Chapter Seven: I'm Going to Need a Kleenex.	*36*
Chapter Eight: Morning Announcements, Show and Tell, Talent Shows, and End of the Year Awards	*41*
Chapter Nine: New Kids Are Family Too!	*47*

*Chapter Ten: OK, Elementary Teachers, We Need
          to Get the Ball Rolling.*   *51*

Chapter Eleven: Daily Rewards   *55*

Chapter Twelve: Retirement   *60*

Part Two: The How   **61**

Chapter Thirteen: First Day of School   *63*

*Chapter Fourteen: Daily Schedule or Is
          It Two O'clock Already?*   *71*

*Chapter Fifteen: What Do You Do with the
          Rest of the Kids?*   *76*

*Chapter Sixteen: Grading Papers: How,
          Where and When*   *86*

Chapter Seventeen: Before and After   *99*

*Chapter Eighteen: Teaching to the Test
          (It's Safe and Effective!)*   *105*

*Chapter Nineteen: Classroom Management
          (It Takes More Than an Einstein)*   *116*

Chapter Twenty: I Need a Fix   *128*

Epilogue   *133*

Introduction

This is a book about making connections, genuine connections with your students. And by building a Family within your classroom, you will see how those connections lead to Daily Rewards.

I've included some things that happened over my 18 years teaching in a self-contained Elementary setting. Some are funny. Some might warm your heart, and I've even included some sad moments. But they all have something in common. Every one of these stories happened because of the connections we made. And as a result, the rewards were indeed daily.

Although I retired before the pandemic hit, I believe good teaching leads to good learning. And you can make it happen anywhere. Whether you're standing next to the whiteboard in front of a crowded classroom or sitting alone in your kitchen with your laptop, you can create those connections and build that Family. A real Family.

Part One: The What

Chapter One: Every Teacher Has One. Here's Mine

We had a morning routine. Kids come in, put up their backpacks, turn in their homework, sit down and start the morning warm-up. No talking (We had Chat Time later). After announcements, I would take care of attendance and lunch count. This is when the kids had Chat Time.

I was still sitting at my computer when I felt someone tap my shoulder. Everyone knew not to come into 'my country' until I was finished. So I thought this could be something.

"Mr. Teel, you might want to come see this." I looked up to see one of my kids sitting at his desk with his head down. To his right, on the tile floor was the largest pile of vomit I had ever seen.

"Jimmy, are you OK?" As I was talking to him, I heard the sound of 25 chairs sliding across the floor, then mass gagging. When I looked up, my entire class was pressed against the wall. It looked like they were all standing on the edge of the top floor of the Empire State Building! You couldn't have peeled them off that wall with a crowbar.

"Good Lord. Haven't you guys seen throw-up before?"
"It's the smell!"

"Breathe through your mouth."

"Now I can taste it."

"Somebody call the office!"

Within seconds, the morning custodian came in. "Good Lord! Who let that dog in here?" Although I thought that was a bit amusing, I turned my attention back to the sick boy. He seemed to be feeling better, so I asked him to stand up.

"Were you OK last night! No problems?" I asked.

"No, I was OK last night."

"What about this morning? What did you have for breakfast?"

I heard the young man who had alerted me to the situation in the first place reply in a pretty good English accent, "Apparently he had a blueberry muffin."

By this time Jimmy and I had started to walk toward the classroom door. I must admit that the way the messenger had said 'apparently' made me start to smile.

As we made our way to the door, I heard a tiny, squeaky voice add, "And some sausage."

Chapter Two: Beginnings

I didn't start teaching until I was 43. I think that was an advantage. Being one of the oldest and especially being a man in an Elementary school was like being an 'immediate grandpa figure.' That perception by students and their parents would be a benefit throughout my career. I have nothing but admiration and respect for young teachers coming right out of college and jumping into situations that they were probably not prepared for.

Both of these events happened in my first week of teaching. It was hot. The class was loud. I was trying to feel my way around. I had spent many years coaching young kids in Little League and I had two young boys at home. I found myself teaching first grade. The desks were arranged in the old fashion grid, maybe five rows of five. Out of nowhere, one student started yelling at the top of his lungs, "I want to kill myself!" I looked in that direction and saw him under his desk rocking in the fetal position. I walked over to the wall, pushed the button to the office, asked for the counselor to come down ASAP, (she turned out to be the most amazing educator I would know), and then sent a student across the hall for reinforcements. That teacher gathered up all of my kids and went to the playground leaving me and the screaming little boy alone, hoping for the counselor's quick arrival. I crawled under the desk next to his and said, "Hey, let me tell you what's going on in my life." I don't know how long we laid there on the floor. I was trying my best to deflect and get him to stop thinking about his situation. He actually stopped rocking and yelling and started listening to what I was saying. After a few minutes, things settled down a bit. I'm sure I was boring the heck out of him. And as the counselor walked in, he said in a matter of fact way, "Gee, Mr. Teel. Your life sucks."

That same week it was still hot. I did not have recess that week. Our school was designed to have a little hallway separating two classrooms. In that hallway were two small student bathrooms. I tried very hard not to use it, but I looked at the clock and realized that I only had ten minutes before my kids came back. So I quickly opened the door, stepped in something soft, and began to slide across the tile floor. My body turned completely around and I landed on the john. My back broke the fall (It still bothers me today) I pulled myself up to a sitting position. *What the*...I thought. Someone had actually crapped on the floor!

Then I looked at the bottom of my shoe. It was covered. I wish that I had not worn the waffle-sole shoes that day. I knew time was running short. I felt a trickle of sweat running down my temple. For some reason, I pulled out a pencil from my shirt pocket and tried my best to remove the material from my waffle-sole shoe. I was sweating. I hate sweating! Did I mention it was hot? Why isn't there better ventilation in here? Who designs a bathroom without a window? Did he do that coming in or going out? I sat there on my fourth day of teaching and questioned every decision

I had made in life, especially the most recent one of becoming a first-grade teacher. I must be insane! Time was running out. The shoe would have to do. I stood up, composed myself, threw the pencil in the trash, and waited at the door to greet my students. As they filed by, I stared at each and every boy. "Which one of them was it?" I still have my suspicions.

Both stories have their Rewards. In the first one, the young man and I developed a sense of trust and caring for each other. And actually, the year turned out pretty good for both of us. I know what you're thinking. What in the world is the Daily Reward in the second story? Well, I have been able to tell that story at every family event and dinner party for the last 20 years.

It was so worth it.

Chapter Three: The Power of a Triangle

The teams have changed. When I was growing up, parents and teachers were on one side and kids were on the other. Now, it's teachers versus the kids, the parents, and sometimes even our own administrations. I can remember sitting at the table for a parent conference and literally sitting in the little chair looking at my teacher AND my parents across the table (Spanish Inquisition) Now the Teacher is sitting alone.

You can change that. By building relationships (connections) with your students AND their parents, you can drastically reduce the daily stress in your classroom and subsequently in your life. You read that right. I said AND their parents. Throughout the rest of this book, I will show you how it can be done. With some more stories. Let's get started.

Architects and structural engineers understand the strength of a triangle. It can be just as powerful in education. Think of the three points of a triangle representing the Student, the Teacher, and the Parent. Think of the lines between those points as connections or bonds or relationships. The stronger those bonds the easier your life will be. The goal is to make all three of those lines strong, genuine connections. Based on my years in elementary classrooms, it is possible to have a good year with just one of those connections (Student to Teacher). But when you add a strong connection between the Student and the Parent, your odds of success increase considerably. If you can build the hardest one (the line between Teacher and Parent), you are almost guaranteeing success.

There is a wall between most teachers and parents, I'm sure there are many reasons for this. A lot of this is based on each person's individual history, misconceptions, fears, anxieties. Whatever. But I promise you. When you build that powerful triangle, you will see a dramatic change in the educational, emotional, and social success of all three players! That sounds like a visionary's 'Pie in the Sky' beginning of the year speech. But it translates into a calmer classroom that both you and your students will actually want to be in, no nasty e-mails from uninformed parents, maybe even some 'Joy and Laughter.' You will see tangible changes in your life when you are not constantly thinking, "I hope Jimmy doesn't go home and tell that mom of his what I said in class, or actually ducking into the next aisle over in the grocery store when you see Jimmy's mother." Every morning I would get to class early and do my stretches on the little rug in my class library. I used to ask myself, "Is there any place in the world I would rather be than here." I told myself if I answered yes, I would quit.

I'm not naive. I realize many parents are not involved in their kids' education. Maybe not even involved in their life. So that one line in the triangle might not exist at all. After a few frustrating years, I would sometimes pretend that some of my kids didn't even have a mom or dad. And some were being raised by wolves!

That's why I would treat the kids in my classrooms just like they were my own. Starting from day one.

I started working on building that line between Teacher and Parent even before school started. I would actually call each home of the kids on my class list. I got a hold of a girl in my upcoming third-grade class and introduced myself. I could hear her mom calling, "Who is it, Honey?" The little girl answered, "It's my teacher and he's a boy!" That turned out to be a really strong triangle. Would I be able to contact every parent? Of course not, but today it is even easier to communicate with all the options available. I know some parents wouldn't respond or even care. I get it. I am not a visionary. I am an old grizzled realist. But I made an instant connection with some of those kids and their parents and we talked it up in class. We normalized the relationship between Teacher and Parent and those kids who weren't lucky enough to be living that life heard about, saw it, and I'm sure craved it. Kids get it. They can see what other kids have. Even if it's the minority of the kids in that particular classroom. I remember one day a student was helping me clean the whiteboard. It was the cleanest in the school! Out of the blue, he said, "I sure hope I don't grow up to be like my dad." Kids say things like that when they feel comfortable and safe. That's the power of building connections based on trust and caring.

That was a Daily Reward! Maybe our conversation would help shape his future life as a father.

Chapter Four: How to Get Parents on Board and How to Have a Successful Year Even If They Don't

Having a Parent's Night is the first and most important step in knocking down that wall. If your school doesn't have one, beg, barter, and plead. It is an opportunity to not only preview the year but to 'humanize' yourself.

They won't admit it, but most parents are afraid of teachers. Most teachers won't admit it, but they are afraid of parents. When you have the chance to show them that you are a real person with real feelings and a real life, things get a whole lot easier. I remember walking through the grocery store in my shorts, pushing the cart when I ran into a student of mine. He said, "Mr. Teel, I didn't know you had legs!"

Then his little brother said, "And he's got beer!"

I had already made a good connection with the parents, so I replied, "I need a beer after the day we had."

The parents laughed and said something like, "Are you sure that's enough."

I actually had one of my Parent Nights catered. It was great. You should have seen the looks on the parents' faces when they walked in. Right away they knew this was going to be an interesting year. I had a 20-foot-long whiteboard in that classroom, and it was filled with everything they needed to know. Not only was the daily schedule up, but all of the major events of the year were posted. I even posted every job I had ever had on one end of the board, my wife's name, and my sons' names and ages. 'Humanize.'

I started the night this way. "Thanks for coming, I have a piece of butcher paper with three lists of five numbers on it. I want all of you to visit and discuss the five things you expect this year. Then I want you to list the five things you expect from your child, and finally, list the five things you expect from me. Not what you would like, but what you expect. When you are finished, come get me. I will be outside the door."

When I came back into the room, we reviewed the lists, discussed them, and then I said, "Here are the five things I expect this year." Here is where being the old grandpa figure became an advantage. Everyone listened and we realized that our lists were very similar. I then told them that I would treat their kids as if they were my own. Then I added, "If you are not comfortable with that, I understand."

"Please visit with my principal and she can move your child into another room. No hard feelings." Not one parent took that offer. We then talked about my 'Open Door Policy.' I want parents in my room. I want them to see what the real world is like. I want them to see what little Jimmy and Sally do in class each day. I want parents to see me as a real person who knows what he is doing, who is passionate about teaching, and who genuinely cares about their kids. And I want them to get involved and help.

I used rotations in my classroom two to three days a week. I needed help so I recruited parents to man the stations. I would show them what I wanted and set up the rotations so that I would have some time to float to help as needed. The kids loved it! And the more we did it, the parents became comfortable and we covered a bunch of material. I had one girl tell me at the end of the year that she felt like she had gone through two years of school. We also had parents come in for our Read-a-Loud sessions. They were classrooms filled with 'Joy and Laughter.' All parents were invited. Not all could or wanted to help, but the kids appreciated them and they started to view this collaboration as normal. The kids whose parents did not help would actually go home and try to persuade their moms and dads to come to school. And even if those parents never showed up, their kids absolutely loved and benefited from having other moms and dads in the classroom.

The Power of a Triangle.

Chapter Five: Parent/Teacher Conferences. Be the Expert in the Room.

Every once in a while my mind would drift while I was giving a direct teach. I would look out at my class and count what I considered the 'normal' students based on certain criteria. Then at recess, I would ask other teachers if they ever did things like that. Soon after those conversations my class and I would be walking down the hall and pass an oncoming class. The teacher would flash a hand signal somewhere between two and five.

Have you ever been talking to one of your students and wondered how in the world can a ten-year-old have this many quirks and misconceptions? Then when you meet the parents you say to yourself, "There you go," within the first minute.

When I first started teaching. I would have to redirect two, maybe three kids during the day. When I retired there would be two, maybe three that I didn't have to redirect. Let's be honest. A lot of parents aren't doing a very good job of raising their kids. Not all. Don't get me wrong. There are still absolutely wonderful parents and guardians out there, teaching responsibility, kindness, and especially empathy. Unfortunately, today teachers are not only responsible for their kids' academics but also for their social and emotional needs. It's hard to get a kid to think about subject pronouns when they are tired, hungry, or even just scared.

We can build that bond with our kids in the classroom. But how do we do it with parents? I realize that the parents who need educating the most rarely show up for conferences. They usually only do when they are upset and want to blame the teacher. But if you can get them to come in, you need to have a plan that will make it a successful use of time.

Most important factor: The teacher has to *Be the Expert in the Room*. You have to be prepared for anything and everything. This is where the Teacher to Student part of the triangle comes into play. I remember sitting in a conference early in my career and a mom asking, "Who does Jimmy play with at recess? Is he eating all of his lunch?"

I didn't know the answers. From that moment on, I vowed to never be in that awkward position again. The next time I walked into a conference room I was going to be the one who held all of the cards.

I started building those connections. I used every part of the daily schedule to get to know my kids. Not only their academic strengths and weaknesses, but what they liked to eat, who they played with, what sports they played, did they have any brothers and sisters, what was their favorite movie, TV-show, and just as important, what they didn't like.

Lunch is a treasure trove of information. I started to stay in the cafeteria with my class. Not every day. Maybe three days a week. We all need downtime. Each day we would walk down the hall to the cafeteria. I tried to use that time to get to know my kids a little better. We had a line leader and a helper each week. We didn't talk out of respect for the other classes. But I have to admit that I occasionally engaged in whispered conversations with the front of the line. When we got to the cafeteria, I supervised the kids as they made their way through the food line. 'Please' and 'Thank You' were required of all. We talked about how hard the cafeteria people worked and that they deserved to be treated with respect. After a week or so, the first thing I heard when we got our food was "Mr. Teel, sit with me, sit with me." We all took turns. I usually ate everyone's peanut butter and jelly sandwich bones. I saved a lot of money on lunches. We had great conversations: funny, interesting. But mostly I sat there and listened.

Recess is another place to just listen, sometimes, I would play basketball or soccer with the kids. On the first day of school in later years, I made it a tradition to go down the slide. You should have seen the faces of the kids AND the teachers as grandpa climbed up the ladder and slid down to the bottom (Without hurting myself) Watch and listen. No controlling, no structure. Just being a minor part of their very important free time.

Before school, after school, in the bus and car lines. Listen, listen, listen.

Back to the conference. Know and provide concrete evidence of the student's reading level, words per minute, self-correcting techniques. Do they go back and repeat before a word they aren't sure of? Details. Do they drop ending sounds? Do they drop short words such as: and, the, or? Do they add little words? How strong is their comprehension? Can they summarize? Provide the same material for Writing, Math, and test-taking skills. Be the Expert in the Room. Know what the problem is before you go in. Anticipate every question and statement you might hear from the parents. And, oh yeah. You know who Jimmy plays with at recess, and if he is finishing his lunch.

I would welcome the parents as they came in. Introduce myself and the first thing out of my mouth was "This is not going to be a bad conference." I would state the problem by saying, "This is what I'm seeing in my classroom," without any value judgement whatsoever.

Then I would say, "Jimmy is your son. You know him better than I do. What can I do? I need your help." Then I would stop talking, sit back in my chair, and WAIT for them to respond. Another advantage of being the old Grandfather. But you can do it too. You can take control of the situation. Lay everything out, stop talking and sit back. You have just put the ball back in their court. When I saw an opening, I would tell the parents that my classroom is always open, and I would love for them to come help teach the kids. Wow! You should see the blank looks. You can hear a pin drop. Then the stammering starts about how they work all the time and really can't take any days off. You are starting to hold all of the cards. If you have kids of your own, you can bring up the fact that you have been on the other side of the table.

"Believe me, I get it." Then I'd mumble something like, "Those kids of mine." Humanize. You're breaking the wall down. You're building the Triangle.

If you don't have any kids of your own, be ready for it. It's usually their trump card. "Well, tell me, Miss Smith. Do you have any kids?"

Here is what you say. "No. We haven't been blessed yet, but I nurture, teach, and love 30 kids a day. We laugh, we cry, we grow as we learn. I've been doing this for six years, so I have 180 kids." It's even better if you are Departmentalized and teach six sections a day. Let's see. That's maybe 125 kids a year for six years. You get the idea.

Seriously, sincerely invite them to come and watch what you do. They will either accept the offer and become supporters, or decline and accept the fact that You are the Expert in the Room.

Just a thought: The response above is one of the very few advantages of teaching in a departmentalized setting. Just saying.

Chapter Six: I Love That Kid!

We had a routine in our classroom. A daily routine. A weekly routine. It creates consistency and stability. I always said, "If you can read the board you will have a great year." Everything we were planning to do for that segment of time was listed on the board. We started off each day with the morning menu. It would usually have a review of some sort, something we were working on that week, and usually something silly.

One of my traditional first-week menu items was "Illustrate a Mattayu." I told the kids not to talk or ask any questions, just do the best you can. "We will go over it in a minute." We always went over it.

So, on this particular morning, I walked around the room watching how the kids were handling the illustration part. Some got their colors out and were really getting into it. Others were scrunching their faces, and some were just staring. I gave it a few minutes (Morning menus were short and sweet) Finally, a student blurted out, "Mr. Teel, what's a mattayu?" I paused for a bit (Comedy timing).

Then I answered in my best New Jersey accent, "Nuthin, what'sa matta you?" Most of the kids cracked up.

A few continued to stare. Laughter is a great way to start the day.

Building that connection between Teacher and Student takes time. You must start with a strong foundation, then add to it each and every day. Kids get it. They know who the teachers are who really want to be there. I can walk into a classroom and get a sense of the environment immediately. Even if the room is empty. I can actually feel the warmth of some teachers' rooms. It might be how they set it up or what's on the walls. It's tangible. It's all about the Teacher. On the other hand, I can walk into a classroom and feel nothing. It feels cold and uninviting. Kids respond in safe, comfortable settings. They can be themselves, open up, and grow.

I love it when kids can make me laugh. I am not one who laughs out loud. I usually just smile and acknowledge the remark. That would change. I had a student in my class who was smaller than most, usually reserved with his fellow classmates. But for some reason, he came alive in my class, and I am so glad he did. Most of the time he would talk in an emphasized, slow Texas drawl. Picture Robert Duval in the third grade.

At the beginning of the year, I explained to my class that my desk area with my computer was 'my country.' The rest of the classroom was 'their country.' They were not allowed in 'my country' for any reason. No exceptions. I even choreographed the concept by standing up in my area and saying, 'my country.' Then stepping over the imaginary line and saying, 'your country.' I did that for at least 15 seconds to make my point.

One morning while the class was working on the menu, I was in 'my country' sending in attendance and the lunch count. I heard something, then felt someone breathing on my right neck and shoulder. I looked up to see this young man just staring at me. I said in a quiet, restrained voice, "My country, Get out." Then I went back to what I was doing. Just seconds later, I felt the same warm breath on the left side of my neck. I turned slowly and the young Robert Duval said, "I got a veeeza for your kuuunntry." I looked him right in the eye and smiled.

Immediate, genuine, lasting connection. I laughed out loud when I told the story at the dinner table.

I love that kid.

We covered more than academics in my class. We talked about virtually everything that would impact their lives. I tried to bring the real world in. I'm sure you know that a lot of these kids don't have a clue as to how to be a person. It's not their fault. Most are not being mean-spirited. They just don't know. We used to go over the very basic elements: How to walk into a classroom, how loud your voice should be, how to eat, how to drink without making noises, how to treat each other, and if you burp or pass gas, have the common decency to say excuse me. We called it 'Class and Style.' Well, we did make some progress. Some, more than others. For those who weren't quite getting it, I came up with an idea. I was going to start a Camp Teel where kids could learn all the basic tenets of being a person. It would be in the summer and it would run 125 dollars a week. During the school year when I noticed we weren't making as much progress as I had hoped, I would suggest to certain students that they should attend Camp Teel this summer.

I even told one student, "Jimmy, tell your parents you can come for free."

One day I was in the middle of a direct teach when the kid with the veezza asked out of nowhere in his old man, Texas accent, "Mr. Teel, Do you have stall bathrooms at camp Teel?"

Before I could answer, he added, "I gotta have a door on migh stawl." Of course, most of us knew camp Teel was not real. I laughed out loud.

When I first started teaching, I noticed a lot of teachers had chairs or stools at the front of their classrooms. Some of the older ones even had rocking chairs. I thought to myself that I would never teach sitting down. I'm high energy. I've got to be moving. I found a blue stool in the closet of my third-year classroom. I spent hours teaching from that stool.

When we had a few minutes to fill, I would share some of my wisdom. We talked about our favorite foods. The subject of vegetables came up. "Ew, I hate vegetables," said the majority. I explained why you need veggies in your diet. Then I shared one of my secrets. When I was a kid and I didn't like something my mom made (we did discuss how eating dinner together every night was important), after taking a bite, I would pretend to cough. Then bring my napkin up to wipe my mouth. Then very discreetly (add new vocab) spit it into the napkin. Then toss the napkin away. To make sure that I would get away with it successfully, I would volunteer to clean the plates and take out the garbage. End of story. I don't remember how much longer it was after sharing this vital information, that we had a parent night or some kind of school event. One of my best moms ever came up to the small group I was talking with. She told everyone how much her two kids loved being in Mr. Teel's class and how every kid should have the opportunity to share the Mr. Teel experience. Then she said that she needed to get home, so I walked her out.

As we got to the door, she turned toward me and said, "Oh, by the way. We use linen napkins." That mom and her husband had a great relationship with their kids. I had built a genuine connection with her kids. I loved her kids. The parents could see that. They trusted me.

The Power of a Triangle.

Chapter Seven: I'm Going to Need a Kleenex.

Reading was the centerpiece of all my classrooms. Reading was everywhere. We had the weekly story from our Anthology series. There were sets of guided reading books. We went to the school library once a week to check out books.

We had our own classroom library with at least 500 titles. In addition to our Science and Social Studies textbooks, we read four Chapter books during each school year. We treated them as Read-a-louds. The kids understood how important Reading was in their lives.

I loved the Read-a-Louds. I enjoyed using different voices for the different characters, speeding up and slowing down, adjusting the volume. And kids need to hear what a well-written book sounds like. We would read two chapters a day. Most of the time I read, but sometimes the kids would read to themselves. At the end of each reading, the kids would answer two questions from each chapter.

One concrete and one abstract. We read books like Shiloh and Charlotte's Web.

I especially liked Because of Winn-Dixie. I saved it for the last book of the year. The kids were more mature and had experienced the importance and joy of reading. The class loved it. Each time I finished reading for the day, they actually pleaded, "One more, one more."

I will never forget that one year when we read the last chapter of Winn-Dixie. I don't know why I struggled with the last page. I had read the book several times before. Maybe it was because I knew this was the last day of read-a-louds. I don't know. The kids picked up on it. I gathered myself and finished the last sentence. I sat there on my blue stool. You could have heard a pin drop. Then one of my kids got up and walked toward me. I stood up. She didn't say a word. She just hugged me. Seconds later two more kids came up and hugged the two of us. A few more, then more. Not a rush, but a slow trickle, which became a steady stream until the entire class was engaged in a complete group hug. Still, not a sound. It was one of the most amazing moments in my life. I still get goose bumps.

We all know teaching is a roller coaster ride. The highs and the lows. I tried to be as level and consistent as possible throughout my career. One year was more difficult than the others for a myriad of reasons. I had lived through several different careers before teaching, so I never really thought about doing it forever. I started questioning myself. My morning stretching routine wasn't as positive as before. I sat down one morning and wrote a short letter of resignation and put it in my desk drawer. Well, maybe a month later we had a difficult morning, so at conference time I brushed my hair, checked myself in the mirror, and opened my drawer. I picked up the letter and started walking toward the door. I knew my principal would be in her office. For some reason, I thought I had better check my e-mail.

I logged in and saw a familiar name. A name I had not seen or thought of in a few years. I opened it. It was from a former student. Maybe five years had passed. He started out by saying hello and that I probably didn't remember him. He told me where he was living and that he was OK. Then…He said that he hadn't had a teacher like me since he left our school. He said that I was different. Then the one sentence that changed my decision and my life. This former student of mine said that I was the only teacher he had ever had who listened to him. I sat there quietly for a while, closed my desk drawer, grabbed a Kleenex, and walked down the hall to pick up my kids.

I tossed the letter.

I didn't always teach in a self-contained classroom. One year I taught five sections of fifth grade science. I remember doing a direct teach right after lunch. Everyone is a bit sluggish during that period. I was at the front of the room. Still had the blue stool, but that day I was actually standing up. It was a large classroom. The door was a good forty feet in the back. While I was talking, I noticed someone standing in the doorway looking at me. It was a teenage boy. Very fit. He looked like a high school athlete. He started to walk toward the front of the room. I didn't recognize him until he was about 20 feet away. I couldn't believe that this was the same little boy I had taught in the third grade years before. I remembered him when he was going through incredible challenges in his young life. And even though he was small and fragile back then, he was the most determined and positive kid I had ever known. His mother had helped in the classroom even after her son had moved on to the fourth grade. We had a strong connection. He walked right up to the front of the room and hugged me so hard I couldn't breathe. I couldn't believe that this was the same kid. My class sat and watched. They didn't know what to think. I heard someone ask.

"Who is that?" Then, "I think it's his son."

They weren't completely wrong.

It was the last week of school. It had been a good year. We had looped with this class so we had been together for two years. This student had been my 'Right Hand' for both years. It's not an appointed position. She just naturally assumed the role. She kept me on schedule, reminded me what CAMP class we were supposed to be in that day, and knew the lunch menu. Generally, she made my job a whole lot easier. Her mother helped out in class and field trips and was there to pick her daughter up. We shared the same philosophy. This was a powerful Triangle. Right before they left, we started talking about the whole year, and that we couldn't believe it was almost over. It started to get a little emotional. They stood up to leave. But right before we got to the door, my number one assistant stopped and hugged me.

For the past two years, we had enjoyed a relationship filled with good-natured teasing, back and forth bantering, and lots of laughing. But mostly mutual respect. I couldn't resist.

I said, "You know, if I had a daughter, I would want her to be just like you." She tightened her hug. Then I added, "Well, maybe not JUST like you."

She loosened her hug and said, "Thank you for ruining what could have been a very special moment." We all needed a Kleenex. We were laughing so hard.

Loved it!

Chapter Eight: Morning Announcements, Show and Tell, Talent Shows, and End of the Year Awards

I was lucky enough to work for one of the best school districts in Texas. We had a unique way of starting each day. Everyone would meet in the gym for the morning announcements. After The Pledge of Allegiance, we would take care of daily business. Then we would sing. What an incredibly positive way to start the school day. I can still hear over 500 kids singing "I Believe I Can Fly." And you know what? They believed it. That was also the first time I can remember hearing about Richard Stands.

Things change and for some reason, we stopped going to the gym. We went back to having morning announcements in our classrooms. But the neat thing was that each class took turns doing them for the rest of the school year. We rotated every week. Well, that was right up our alley. There were certain things you had to cover, but then you had about five minutes to entertain the masses.

We had an interesting group of individuals that year. One boy had the habit of blurting out random thoughts as I was teaching (Not the young Robert Duval) One time during a mini-lesson I heard from out of the blue, "Old man got somethin' to saaay." In an old man's voice.

Another time it was, "China Sea's got a good buff-aay." I don't know why, but he would always drag out that last syllable. I could tell it was annoying the class even though I found it to be amusing. I made a deal with the 'old man.' He could blurt out only once a day (it better be good). And in exchange, he could do a comedy bit every Friday during Show and Tell. He accepted.

Why am I sharing this story? When I found out about the change in the morning announcements, I immediately thought what a great idea for a radio sketch. So every day of our week, right after the pledge, it was time for something we called, "Old man got something to say." (Yes, I borrowed the idea from SNL) Each day we would do a segment about how things used to be. I remember this one.

He's doing this in his old-man voice. "When I was in school, we didn't have no fancy physical education with your fancy climbing walls, and your bows and arrows, and those little cups you try to stack up on each other." No sir! We had gym class with a big red ball! You threw it at each other and we liked it! His status in the classroom was elevated immediately and our connection was cemented for the rest of the year. Certainly a Reward.

I know most teachers think that Show and Tell is a thing of the past. But it's a great way to teach oral skills and how to stand in front of a group of people without throwing up. Oh yeah. The kids like it and at times can be very funny. I remember one student asked if he could bring in his electric keyboard. He had been taking piano lessons and thought it was time to show what he knew he could do. Well, he started playing a piece that sounded pretty difficult to me. He was actually playing quite well. As a matter of fact, he played it so well that when he stopped and brought his hands up, the music kept playing!

The other part of Show and Tell is the Tell. After all the showing, I would ask if anyone had a Tell. To be honest, sometimes I would get a little distracted and didn't give my complete attention to the Tells. Putting out fires and all. After this one girl finished her story, the class applauded and we moved on. Well, the following Friday she had another Tell and I guess I was putting out fires again. Halfway through her story, another girl whispered to me, "This is the same story she told last week." I wasn't completely convinced, but I was going to pay more attention. The next Friday she said that she had a Tell, got up, and seemingly told the exact same story.

I said, "Do you know that you keep telling the same story?"

"I like that story."

My favorite Tell. One of my third grade girls said she had a Tell about her mother, that she wasn't feeling well, and as a matter of fact was in the hospital right now, "Getting her uterus yanked out!"

Next!

I'm pretty sure we started putting on a year-end talent show at the end of my very first year. We had one each of the next 17 years. We started auditions with about three weeks left in the school year. Anyone could try out. Not everyone wanted to, but we did encourage them. The kids who chose not to perform worked behind the scenes as music directors, stage hands, and ushers. I picked the most organized of that group to be the director. We also needed people to design and print programs and draw posters for the hallway. Everyone participated. It was quite a project. More like organized chaos. The kids worked hard, and it actually came together just in time. We had a Master of Ceremony and the crew kept all of the acts in order and on time. There were singers and dancers, musicians, magicians, gymnasts, and even some stand-up comedians. You should have seen the young Robert Duvall's set. It was hilarious. The whole class joined together for the finale. We always ended the show with Taylor Swift's, Love Story. I'm not sure why, but it worked. The response from parents and siblings was fantastic. I counted over 80 people in my classroom one year. The shows were an amazing culmination of the daily development of genuine relationships between Teacher and Student, Parent and Teacher, and Parent to Student. It was nice to end each year on such a high note.

We also held an in-class Awards ceremony at the end of each year. Each and every kid received a personal award based on the events of the year. There weren't any Best, or Class Clown, or Most Athletic. These awards were carefully thought out. Sometimes it would take weeks of replaying the year over in my head to come up with some of them. I know, sad. But real. And somehow things always worked out. Some of the awards were: One in a Million, No Make That Two, Right Hand Man, Best Answers to Unasked Questions, the Who Knew Award, and the Golden Boy (only given this one once. His mother yelled out from the back of the room, "You nailed it!") The Oscar of the awards was the 'Solid' award. It was given to the student who wasn't necessarily number one academically but was kind, generous, and responsible. The type of person who was always pleasant and actually fun to be around. The kids who received the 'Solid' award were genuinely affected. It had built a reputation over the years and it meant something to receive it. Even the parents were aware of it. The classroom was packed for these celebrations of each other. One mom, who had not been able to be as involved as she wanted during the year (she took care of her children and worked), said the ceremony and the interaction between all of the students were 'phenomenal.' There was one student who received something extra with his award. He was the epitome of a young, good ole boy. Complete with boots, cowboy hat, and a thick Texas drawl. He was a great kid. He actually fixed the barstool that I now taught from, (had to leave the blue one behind) when it needed tightening. He even brought his own tools. Throughout the year he would raise his hand, and without fail, declare, "I have two things." And he did. Whether it was a statement or a question. Well, I couldn't resist. His award was the coveted 'I Have Two Things' award.

As he walked up to the front of the room, I announced, "I have two things. Number one: He asks some of the best questions ever, and two, girls, he's single." I am not making this up.

Almost on cue, and completely in sync, the class started singing, "You don't have to be lonely at Farmersonly.com." Everyone roared, including the young man. We laughed until we cried.

Another great way to end the year. The class had paid attention to each other and was indeed, a Family.

Chapter Nine: New Kids Are Family Too!

If you want to know what's going on in your school, sit in the teacher's workroom for a few minutes. Decisions made by the Administration somehow make it to the workroom within seconds. Even before the advent of the internet. And new student arrivals? Oh my God. That news sweeps through the school like a wildfire. All the newbie's information (both academic and behavioral) are being discussed before the first morning bus arrives. But the best part is how everyone knows what teacher is getting the new addition. You should see the feeling of relief on the unaffected teachers' faces.

Being a new student is challenging for the kid, but it is also tough on the teacher and the class. It changes the whole dynamic of the classroom. And WHEN the new student arrives makes a major difference. If it's early in the year, acclimation for all is smoother. But when a new kid arrives halfway through the school year. Yikes!

Early one morning, almost immediately after announcements, there was a knock on my door. I walked over to see who it was. The kids were working on the morning menu. I opened the door, and standing there was the school secretary and a young girl. Before the secretary could say anything, the little girl blurted out, "I'm yours!"

For some reason, I didn't say a word. I just stood there and stared at her. I think it was the way she introduced herself. I felt the blood rush from my face. My knees got weak. I can only imagine what the secretary was thinking. Then I started to process everything. She said she was mine. She is probably ten. Where was I ten years ago? What was I doing? Was I dating anyone? It was still a blur.

Finally, the secretary rescued me. "Mr. Teel, this is Sally. She is your new student."

"Oh."

At the end of the day, I went to the office to explain to the secretary what had happened to me. She cracked up. I then asked her if from now on, she could give me at least a 15-minute heads up before she brought me a new student. From then on, I kept a spare desk with a number line and a blank name tag already taped on and ready to go. All I had to do was grab a sharpie and write the new name. Then set up the desk. I think it made the new student feel a bit more welcomed, like part of the family. Less stress for everyone. Especially me.

The message is that your students become your Family the very first day. No matter what day of the school year.

Some new kids blend in better than others. Some are quiet, soft-spoken, and some blow in like a Hurricane!

Picture a young Jim Carrey. Same body movements, same voice. Exact same facial expressions. I remember the morning he blew in. I knew he was coming. I made it my practice not to read student files before I met them. I did not want to make any prejudgments. I would find out later that his folder was quite substantial. As soon as he walked in, I made the Jim Carrey connection. He was amusing and certainly not shy. It was time for recess, so the class lined up as usual: Line leader first, then helper. The young Carrey decided he would immediately make his presence known and jumped in line ahead of the leader. It was his first day so I decided not to make it an issue. We opened the door and started to make the short walk to the playground. About ten feet outside the classroom, he dropped to the floor, wrapping his arms tightly around my leg (Like a python) I continued to walk down the hall. It was more like sliding down the hall, dragging Jim each step of the way. I acted like this was perfectly normal and didn't faze me in the least. My class followed my lead and paid no attention to the unusual hallway procession.

Right before we got to the outside door, Jim said, "Hey Mr. Teel, did you know I was actually kicked out of my old school?"

"No shit!"

I'm not sure if I said it out loud. I had never come close to saying anything inappropriate before. Maybe it was just in my head. I'm pretty sure it crossed the minds of some of my students. The young Jim Carrey released his death grip, jumped up, and ran straight for the swings.

It was an up and down year for us. But I think we both benefited by the end of the year. He did make me laugh. One day he walked into the room with his jacket tied around his waist.

"What's up?" I asked. He said he wanted to know what it would be like to be a girl, so he was going to try it for the day. Later as we were getting ready for dismissal, I noticed that he didn't have the jacket around his waist anymore. "How did it go?"

"I don't want to be a girl. Not one person held the door open for me."

We developed a pretty good connection. We sat together every Friday for Show and Tell. His whispered critiques of each act were hilarious. We talked. There was trust. I think he was happy.

Whether it's low or high maintenance, everyone needs to be included.

Family.

Chapter Ten: OK, Elementary Teachers, We Need to Get the Ball Rolling.

I think most teachers would agree that what we're doing in education ain't working. The system is broken. And if a system is broken, then some or all of the components in that system are broken, too. However, I truly believe that the top 10 to 20 percent of students in our current system will succeed no matter what. That is a tribute to the triangle line between Student and Parent. But what can we do for the rest of our kids?

I was an Elementary teacher for 18 years. I still consider myself an Elementary guy. I can't imagine teaching the upper levels. Middle School and High School teachers are amazing. I know if I taught High School, my family would have to visit me in prison.

Elementary Schools have to start the process of change. We must build a better Foundation. We need to have that image of the Triangle in the back of our minds in everything we do. We have to keep trying to build those genuine connections of the Triangle each and every day. If we have all three, we can send our kids to Middle School with a great deal of confidence that they will be successful. I am a realist. But I firmly believe that our kids will be successful even with just two of those connections. And if we develop a truly strong bond of trust and caring, one of those lines is enough. When we send our 5th graders on to Middle School, they need to have a strong foundation. Not just academically, but socially, and emotionally. If we have to pretend they don't have parents, so be it. We have to provide a classroom environment where kids feel comfortable and safe. They have to want to be there. It has to enhance or be the students' family. And I strongly believe that 'if a kid's not laughing, he's not learning.'

We have to go back to self-contained classrooms. Young kids need stability. They need to be able to come to school each day and know what to expect and to know what's expected of them. That Teacher needs to provide the Family that is missing in a lot of our kids' lives.

Stability. Consistency. No surprises. Kids need that anchor in their lives. Self-contained Elementary schools through grade five can provide that if everyone is on board. I know all of the arguments against it. "What if you have a student that you really can't mesh with?"

"I'm not good at Math." Those statements usually come from teachers who haven't done it or haven't given it a chance when they were self-contained. Most teachers don't mesh with every one of their students whether they are self-contained, team-teaching, or part of a departmentalized group. If I have the same group of students all day, every day we start building connections. But the teacher has to put in the work. I have already shared how I did it. Use your daily schedule wisely. Make every minute count. Make those kids yours! The good things and the bad things. After a while, your daily routine will become theirs. Your expectations will become theirs. We got a new student midway through the year. I was floating during Silent Reading and I heard one of my first graders explain to the new kid, "It's OK to fart in Mr. Teel's class, but you have to say excuse me." Family. And your parent and your discipline problems are yours. I don't want to be involved in other teachers' parent and discipline issues. No thank you. Remember being the Expert in a parent conference? Well, you can't be, if you are sharing kids.

I completely understand the other argument about not being great in every subject. And if we were talking about the upper grades, I would agree 100 percent. But we are talking about Elementary School. When a teacher is well-versed in the curriculum, everyone benefits.

One year we looped my third graders to fourth grade. Wow! We hit the ground running on the first day of school and never looked back. At the end of the year standardized test, eighty-six percent of my students scored Commended in Math. We were able to do that because I knew the strengths and weaknesses of each one of my kids and we planned our lesson plans based on that. Connections, Triangles.

There are some great school districts out there doing wonderful things. There are great teachers and parents doing everything they can to make sure their kids have every opportunity to be successful. But I think most educators would agree that we face incredible obstacles each and every day from limited funding to lack of parental involvement and student behavior.

We Elementary teachers need to send our kids to Middle School with not only all of the academic tools they need but with the emotional and social skills that will set them up for success. In plain English, we have to produce nice people. I have never been a fan of character programs or classes. It just doesn't make sense to me to say, "OK class, today we are going to learn how to be kind. Tomorrow we are going to teach you how to be honest." It doesn't feel genuine.

In a self-contained classroom, all of those traits that we want our kids to have are treated as normal. Humanize. We model what we do because that's just the way it is. We had one rule in my classroom: Be nice.

Chapter Eleven: Daily Rewards

We talked about how to make connections. How do you know you've made one? How do connections reveal themselves? Your connections will be evident by the way your students treat and react to you. Your Daily Rewards are the result.

I started my teaching career later than most. I was thirty-five years older than the students in my first class. One day I picked up my class after Art. They had made cards for their moms. The line leader showed me the one she had made. I told her it was beautiful and that I thought I would make one for my mother. She looked up at me and said, "Your mother is still alive?"

I used to wear a white shirt and sweater vest during the colder months. Someone had bought me a beige, bulky one for Christmas. I hesitated to wear it because, for some reason, it looked like a woman's sweater. Weeks went by, it was cold. I had worn every other sweater in my closet, so I pulled the beige one out, put it on, and made my way to school. We were doing rotations that morning. Groups of four or five would come to my table to read together. There was one kid in the last group who reminded me of a young Gilbert Gottfried, a comedian with a scrunched-up face and abrupt, loud delivery. His group had been at my table for a while. I couldn't help but notice him staring at me with this deep, thoughtful look on his scrunched-up face. Finally, out of nowhere, he half-shouted, "Mr. Teel, is that a woman's sweater?"

I knew it!

One year I taught third grade in one of those mobile classrooms. It was small but quiet. No hall traffic. One good thing was we had our own bathroom. One bad thing was we had our own bathroom. We were a Family, so when a kid had to use the restroom, they would give me a little wave. I would nod. No big deal (We had bathrooms for both boys and girls) One day we were doing a pretty vocal rapid-fire review. The kids were shouting out answers. A lot of energy. It was fun. After one question, I heard an answer that was a bit louder than the others. Then another one. I couldn't tell who was shouting out the correct answers. I asked another question, the same result. We all stopped for a second, looked at each other. Then we all focused on the boys' restroom. One of my favorite kids of all time was shouting out the answers while sitting in the bathroom!

Now that's feeling safe and comfortable in your environment.

I remember teaching a mini-lesson one day. The young Robert Duvall was in the audience. About halfway through, in his best old-man Texas drawl he asked, "Mr. Teel, when you were dating, how did you handle rejection?" That made my whole day. I used to wonder how he came up with that stuff. But mostly, I wondered how he picked his spots. Comedy is timing. That year I couldn't wait to get to school.

Now that I think about it, our whole day was snack time. We focused on healthy snacks, but every now and then a pastry item might show up. The expectation was that you had to clean up after yourself. I love Honey Nut Cheerios. I would usually break the box out around 10:00 while I was still direct teaching. Then we would take a quiet break. I tried to provide a little of my cereal to those kids who weren't able to bring their own. I remember sitting at my reading table pouring a little bit into baggies and passing them out. By the end of the year, the kids would come up to my table with their own open baggies. The line would stretch across the room.

"For Pete's sake, let Mr. Teel have some of his own cereal just once."

We looked out for each other. I would float the room while the kids were working on Math. Most would be eating something. As I walked around, the kids would hold up one of the snacks they were eating in the air for me to choose from. I can't imagine what that looked like from the hallway. I did get a note from the mom who used linen napkins. She wanted to thank me for introducing her daughters to Twinkies, Ding-Dongs, and Ho Hos. In hindsight, it sounded a bit sarcastic. On the last day of school that year, we had a party. The kids brought teacher gifts. The usual coffee mugs and 15 boxes of Twinkies.

In Texas, we had end of the year standardized tests. I'm sure all states do. They lasted two days. The policy was that when a student finished their test, they would have to sit quietly or read. The idea, of course, was to be respectful of other students and let them finish their own tests. Our class of ten and eleven-year-olds was fantastic. It was as quiet as a library in the 1950s. I think I was more restless than the kids were. It was just another example of a group of kids becoming a real Family and actually caring about each other. They wanted each other to succeed.

Student connections between each other.

We also had a bunch of doughnuts afterward. So it wasn't much different than a regular day.

One of my students got me a miniature crossbow. It was about five inches long with a strong rubber band that you would lock in place while you loaded your preferred projectile. Those tiny, little marshmallows were perfect. The first time I brought it out was at the end of Silent Reading Time. I loaded it, picked a target, and launched it across the room. It only took a few shots to master. Within a few minutes, tiny marshmallows were landing softly in my students' hair. The kids sitting close to me saw what I was doing and started to laugh quietly. Things started getting louder. The targeted students turned around, realized what was happening, jumped up, and immediately assumed an open mouth, crouched position.

"Mr. Teel. Mr. Teel."

I started firing up a barrage of marshmallows and watched the kids try to catch them in their mouths. It seemed like a logical progression. Well, it was getting pretty loud. I'm sure you could have heard us from the hallway. As the frenzy continued, I noticed the door starting to open. In walked my principal. She looked around, assessed the situation, and without missing a beat, assumed the marshmallow catching position. It was classic. She had also made connections. She was also a member of our Family. That morning we all truly enjoyed a Daily Reward.

Connections…Family…Rewards

My principal actually caught a marshmallow.

Chapter Twelve: Retirement

I remember running into some of my former co-teachers who had recently retired. I was getting close myself. I wanted to know how retirement felt. So I asked them if they missed it. They all said the same thing. "No, they didn't." It made me a little sad. I thought to myself that there is no way I'm going to feel like that. I think I now understand what they meant. Honestly, I do not miss grading papers and although I loved coming up with new ways to teach, I do not miss the actual process of writing lesson plans. I look back on the time I spent in the evenings and on weekends getting ready for the week. Wow.

But I do miss the Daily Rewards. And I miss the building of connections and the realization of those relationships. And I miss Richard.

I miss my kids standing up together each and every morning, delivering with pride and conviction these words, "I pledge allegiance to the flag of the United States of America, and to the republic, for Richard Stands, one nation, under God, with liberty and justice for all."

Part Two: The How

Chapter Thirteen: First Day of School

I worked for school districts that let us come in early to work on our rooms. I not only wanted to take my time and get my room the way I wanted it before the kids got there but before those two weeks of much-anticipated work-shops and in-services. There were a few teachers who took advantage of it, but most would wait and try to squeeze it in during the team-building activities. I loved watching the 30-year veterans take part in the team-building.

"You're kidding me. I need to be in my room. We aren't doing this tomorrow, are we?" I didn't get much out of them either, but it felt great to not be stressing out. I think that's the greatest feeling a teacher can have. Just knowing that you are ready. After struggling through my first couple of years, I learned to make that a priority. Be ready each morning. Prior Planning Prevents Poor Performance. I actually learned that in an in-service! Those two weeks before the school year starts could be and should be used more effectively. Every minute could be designed to make our upcoming year successful. Most of the work-shops felt like time-fillers with not much thought put into them. This is a big problem. Teachers don't have time to waste. This has to be fixed.

I think I changed classrooms nine times in fourteen years. Pros and cons. You can get rid of the stuff you don't use, but somebody needs to develop tape that actually sticks. And Ticky-Tak. What the hell is that? Every year I would put up butcher paper for my word wall. One year it covered an entire wall. Every morning I would open the door and assess the damage. At least half of the word wall would be hanging down and touching the floor. After a while, I got used to it and could put it back up pretty quick. I'm sure I spent 200 dollars on tape that year. It's a good thing I got to school before everyone else. I must confess, there was cursing involved.

One year I was sitting in a work-shop feeling pretty good about everything, watching all the teachers' anxiety, thinking, the Five Ps. And after the information-packed session, I walked down the hallway toward the parking lot. I passed an empty room, smiled a smug smile, and noticed a sign on the wall. It read Mr. Teel. "Well, this can't be right. I just passed my room and it's completely set up. This room is not."

Just then my principal walked up and said, "I need you to move to this room." This was the Friday before the first day on Monday!

I replied, "It would have been nice to have been told a bit earlier." She said that she knew I could handle it.

It took all weekend. My kids helped. At least, the word wall stuck.

I must admit that there is one thing about changing rooms that scared me…the teacher's closet. I hated going in. I didn't even want to touch the door handle. Why is there always an inch of dust on it? My two boys begged me, "Please, Dad. Don't open it! For God's sake, don't go in there!" When I did venture in, my sons would reassure me "We love you, Dad."

If you want to know where curriculum dollars are spent, there you go.

Each year when I opened the door, it was the same thing.

The dust is so thick you can't breathe. And when you turn on the dim, yellowish light, it takes you back to nineteenth-century London. What you find is amazing. Thirty-year-old Spelling books, Handwriting primers, Science textbooks that boldly claim that someday we will put a man on the Moon. The last President mentioned in the Social Studies books was Kennedy. World book encyclopedias (Not whole sets mind you). And why are the S and Ce editions always missing? Piles of loose papers stacked on every shelf. Even old student folders. I thought those were supposed to be turned in. Why do old books and papers smell like that? I'm pretty sure I know where Amelia Earhart is.

I don't think I ever tried to completely reclaim one. After a while, you just ignore them. But every once in a while they come in handy. When a kid was talking too much, "Hey Jimmy, how would you like to clean the closet?"

The week before school starts, everyone is asking the same question: Parents, Teachers, Kids. "Are the class lists out, yet?" And when they are finally posted on the bulletin board outside the office…Oh, my God! It's like the storming of the Bastille! It's like a mob of college kids checking their MCAT scores. I would wait my turn at the back of the crowd, watching the range of emotions as the teachers turned around. I swear I heard sobbing one year.

"Yes, yes, yes. I didn't get Jimmy!"

I'm glad Jimmy's mom wasn't standing there. Although I'm pretty sure she would have understood. The point is: the sooner you know who your kids are going to be, the sooner you can start making connections.

Alright, we've got our room ready. We know who our kids are going to be. Let's start building the Triangle. Let's make those connections that are going to lead to Daily Rewards and success for our students and ourselves. We should look forward to getting up and going to school. Teachers deserve to have good days. I want my new kids to come into the classroom and feel comfortable the very first day. You do that by grabbing that class list and inserting yourself into their lives. And the lives of their parents or guardians. With e-mail, texting, face-time, zoom, and yes, even just your basic phone, there is no excuse to not communicate. If you use Facebook, be a professional. Be a professional. Even if the parents never acknowledge your efforts, you have started to break down the wall that prevents Daily Rewards.

Be a salesman (Because that is what we are). What's the old rule for success in sales? It takes ten pitches to make one sale. Make yourself and your phone number familiar. Even if parents don't answer or reply, they will start to know that it is you on the other end. By the way, familiar and family come from the same word origin. I'm telling you, this works. The involved parents absolutely love it, and it starts to put cracks in the walls of those parents who really don't know how to get involved. And you've got nothing to lose. There's no downside to showing that you actually care.

Finally, it's the first day of school. Kids are coming! Remember, we're talking about Elementary kids and hopefully, you're in a self-contained classroom. And hopefully, we have come through the pandemic. I realize that there are going to be some changes in what we try to do and how we are going to utilize technology during the day and throughout the year. More on technology in the next chapter.

Rule number one: Be Yourself!

Rule number two: Treat these kids just like they are your own (If you don't have any yet, treat them like you think you will someday).

Have your entire first day planned to the minute. I'm not kidding. Prior Planning Prevents Poor Performance. It's better to have too much than not enough. If you're going to greet them in the hall, tell them to come in, find their name, sit down, and read the board. If they can't read, tell them to ask their neighbor to help (There's your first Reading Assessment) From this day until you retire, you will have your morning schedule on the board. Do the same thing at the same time each and every day. Your kids will love knowing what's coming up. One year I had a 3rd-grade girl keep me on schedule. "Mr. Teel, it's time for the Math warm-up.")

Do not. I repeat. Do not attempt to put school supplies away as part of your first day. Ideally, you will have made a connection or two with parents. Have them pick up and store the supplies in the back of the room. You can put them away later. Yes, I know it's more work for you, but it will make for a smoother, more comfortable, and more productive first day. If you don't have any parents to help, have the kids put them in the designated area. Just make sure you have enough pencils and copies of the day's work ready.

When they get settled in, start the day. Show them the room, and explain the importance of the Menu on the board. "If you can read the board, you'll have a great year. If you can't, I'll teach you how." Demonstrate how they should come into the room. Pretend you are a student and actually act out what to do. Be silly.

They love it.

Go over the basics. Restroom, snacks, lining up, getting a pencil (I always had enough sharpened pencils for one day ready. Nothing worse than listening to a kid sharpen a pencil).

Oh, Ticonderogas are the best! Expensive, but worth it. Nothing worse than sharpening a brand new pencil and ending up with a one-inch nub. Except watching and listening to a kid do it.

Go over lunch protocol (Teach them what protocol means) Eat lunch with them. I know what you're thinking. This guy is insane! Maybe…but after a while, you can cut it down to once or twice a week. I actually found that when I didn't go with them, I missed it. Eating lunch with your kids builds connections. The kids realize that you could be in the teachers' lounge, but you have chosen to be with them. That's big. That's a Family. I promise this will lead to Daily Rewards. Your efforts will make your day not only easier but fun.

You are building that Teacher to Student baseline of the Triangle.

I can't emphasize this enough. Don't waste the first day! Yes, I know you have to cover the logistics but make it fun. Firm but fun. Make that first day count. You are setting the tone for the entire year. Plan your day down to the minute. Mix in some instruction with the logistics. Introduce the spelling and sight word lists. I'm serious. Why not? Who wants all that dead time? That's just an invitation for bad behavior. Remember how to control your pacing, and use a soothing, confident voice. When your kids go home after school, and their parents (hopefully) ask them how their first day was, instead of answering, "Fine," or just shrugging their shoulders, they smile.

I have a brother who is two years older than I am. He is probably the smartest person I know. Pros and cons. I always looked up to him, but I had to follow his reputation in school. I remember my first day in Miss Crosetto's tenth grade Honors English class. She was about five feet tall and reminded me of the matriarch of an immigrant New Jersey family. I walked into her room, found a desk as far away as possible, and started looking out the window. I quickly heard an unfamiliar voice say, "Mr. Teel, your brother wouldn't be doing that." That was the hardest class in my life. We had a vocabulary lesson that would take me three to four hours every Sunday afternoon. I loved it. Her expectations became mine. She treated us with respect but preached responsibility.

"Do not be late," was her Eleventh Commandment.

I remember one morning it was pouring down rain. I was in my R.O.T.C. uniform and I was drenched. When I got to her classroom, I turned the handle, and nothing. Locked. I felt an empty feeling in my stomach. I must confess. There was cursing.

I knew the next step, walk down the hall to the office, get a pink slip, and probably an hour of detention. But then, a classmate opened the door. I crept in. My classmates had that look of knowing what was coming. Miss Crosetto's head half-turned in my direction and she said, "Take your seat, Mr. Teel. It's raining quite hard, and I know how unorganized you are." My classmates were stunned. As I walked to my desk, I stole a glimpse at the Matriarch. I swear I saw a half-smile.

Firm but fun.

Chapter Fourteen: Daily Schedule or Is It Two O'clock Already?

Ideally, you are teaching in a self-contained Elementary classroom. Your schedule is your own. This can still work if you are team-teaching with one other teacher. It's more difficult. We talked about the kids being yours, but if your partner has the same ideals and goals as you, it's workable. If you are part of an Elementary Departmentalized program where you teach five sections a day, start looking for a new school district.

I taught in a state where the curriculum for each grade level was decided upon. I'm sure every state is the same. Do your research. Know exactly what your grade level is designed to cover.

Know what is to be introduced, what is to be recognized, and what is to be mastered by the student.

We have all heard 'Make it a teachable moment.' and 'Timing is everything.' Well, every moment in your day is a teachable moment, and if you are self-contained, Timing is not only everything, it's yours!

The morning warm-up menu sets the tone for the whole day. It's the first thing your kids see when they walk into the room. Make it meaningful. No busy work. And don't use a commercial daily warm-up book that has six weeks of pre-planned material. Make up your own that has a connection to what you do in your class. Review last week's work. Hit the stuff you know they haven't mastered. Be silly with some of the assignments. I used to think of mine during my commute to school. You have already trained your kids how to come into the room, hang up their backpacks, turn in their homework, grab a pencil, sit down and start working. They knew that Chat Time would be soon. One year my first-grade class was so good at this, you could have heard a pin drop. If you start your day without a purpose, you'll be fighting 'it' all day long. I can't believe how chaotic a lot of classrooms are right off the bat. No one in those classrooms has a chance. And if you have parents in your room, they see that you use every minute, they recognize the importance of being on time. Your kids will, too. I had a mom tell me that their son, who in the past didn't mind being late, would get up, eat breakfast, brush his teeth, grab his backpack, and stand by the front door. Kids get it.

Put that daily schedule on your wall. Break it down to the minute and include everything from morning announcements to Reading to lunch, recess, Silent Reading to clean-up, and dismissal. And stick to it. Kids love routine. They love stability. They want to know what's coming next. You are building a safe, comfortable environment. I always loved teaching Language/Arts in the morning and Math right after lunch and Silent Reading Time. I would reinforce the big daily schedule with a more detailed menu on the board.

Silent Read: 12:00–12:25

Math warm-up: 12:25

I would put the math warm-up in a stack on my blue stool. After a few weeks of training, the kids would put their books away (We had a procedure for that), go up to the front of the room, grab a warm-up and get busy. One day, they all got to the stool at the same time. It looked and sounded like a shark-eating frenzy! Then my principal walked in. She was a bit taken back and said, "What is going on?"

"They're getting their Math warm-ups," I answered.

"Only in Mr. Teel's class." Then she left.

We would work with Math until 1:30, take another snack break, then hit Science and Social Studies. Some weeks we would flip the two, or do one a week. Remember, you know what you are supposed to cover, and the daily schedule is yours. Play around with it. See what is best for you and your students. It will change from year to year depending on your class list. I did find that I was able to cover more before lunch. I think kids are more receptive, too.

Squeeze every minute of the day. That doesn't mean you are delivering material non-stop. You can also cover a lot during your downtime. Snack time, Chat time, Silent Reading time. You are listening, building trust, talking about the real world, and talking about yourself. If kids know what is important to you, it can become important to them. And most importantly, laughing. I used to sit at my little reading table during these downtimes (I'm old, you know). The kids would gather around, eating, and sharing their snacks. I know, not a good idea. But some of the kids didn't have anything to munch on. Families share. My reading table was not against the wall. There was room to slide between my chair and the file cabinets. One day I was drinking my sweet tea and eating a Ding Dong, when I felt someone behind me, breathing on the top of my head.

"Mr. Teel, did you know you have TWO bald spots?" We all roared. One girl sprayed her juice everywhere.

Joy and laughter are very powerful.

Later, as a time filler, I showed my class how to do a spit-take.

"Hey, do this at dinner tonight. Your mom will love it."

I realize that scheduled and unscheduled events come up. You can plan your instruction around the upcoming assemblies, guest readers, etc. But when you're self-contained you can absorb the fire drills, weather days, behavior issues, booboos, and adjust anyway you want. It takes a little stress out of the equation when you control your schedule.

So, to review. Decide on a daily schedule that works for you, and post it. Then stick to it. Kids love routine. The more you stay on schedule, the more confident you are.

If you're thrown off, so are your students. Learn how to adjust. Roll with the flow! Squeeze every minute of the day, especially in the morning. A quicker pace allows you to slow it down a little after lunch. You'll be surprised how much time you have in the afternoon. Even if it just feels like it. But when you do have an interruption, just cross out the part of the schedule that you lost, and catch up the rest of the week.

After a few years of sticking to a daily schedule, I didn't need a clock. I could pretty much tell what time it was based on what was going on in my classroom. I definitely knew when it was tea and Ding Dong time. Kids are on a schedule, too. I had one student who needed to use the restroom at the exact same time each day (Yes, number 2) Sometimes he would make it to the bathroom, sometimes not. I don't know how many times I would be floating the room, helping with Math, putting out fires, breathing in, and asking myself, "Wow, is it two o'clock, already?"

We got it figured out. No big deal. That's what families do.

Chapter Fifteen: What Do You Do with the Rest of the Kids?

"Oh, right. When am I supposed to get that done?" Sound familiar? True enough.

There is a great deal to cover during the school year, and not very much time. We just talked about using your day as efficiently as possible. Squeeze every minute. Another great way to cover a lot of material is by using rotations. Hang on. Don't panic! I did it every year, even with first graders. It doesn't have to look like a cell block in prison. It does require a lot of planning and prep-time, but the great amount of written work it produces makes grading easier. And you get to know your kids inside and out. And that is the whole idea. Pour yourself a glass of wine, open your mind, and read on.

Rotations or stations is one method of covering a lot of material in a shorter period of time than it would require if you were only teaching whole group. It does not take the place of a direct teach to introduce a concept. But is extremely effective in reinforcing and extending what the kids have already seen. We all know that every kid in your classroom is not on the same academic level. You might have a three-year range or more in one classroom. After you have done your beginning of the year evaluations, you can start making lesson plans geared specifically to the different groups you have. You use the same ideas for each station, you just provide different levels of difficulty. At each station, you post a menu with varied selections. Group the kids any way you want. Play with it. See what works, and what doesn't. Change the line-ups. Keep the same ones for a couple of weeks. It's your schedule, your room.

I only used rotations on Tuesdays, Wednesdays, and occasionally Thursdays. Mondays were reserved for direct teach (usually 15-minute mini-lessons) to introduce new concepts. Mondays were pretty rapid fire. Fridays were used to wrap up writing and assessments. I know, pretty traditional. But routine, routine, routine. You will get really good at what you do, and so will your kids. After a few weeks, the kids get used to the pace. Remember, kids, love routine. They know what to expect. No surprises. It builds confidence, accountability, and connections.

And busy, bustling classrooms have fewer behavior issues.

We usually set up five stations:

My Table
Spelling
Writing
Math
Reading

And the class library for early finishers. Each student had a library folder to record what they read throughout the year (An excellent piece for portfolios and parent conferences).

My Table: the epicenter.

This is the reason you do rotations. The things we accomplished at the little reading table made all of the extra planning and work worth it. We always started out by playing cards as a warm-up. The kids love it and it really grabs their focus. I would throw down two cards in front of each kid, (ideally four to five kids per group) then say 'add' or 'subtract' or both. Later on, we would multiply. Sometimes I would say 'add, plus one' or 'add, minus two.' We would get faster and faster. The pace would reach a feverish pitch at times. Get creative. Add three cards, teach strategies. 'Get to a double.' 'Get to a ten.' Use the lower value cards first, then add the higher ones as they progress (Oh, take out the face cards). cards should only take about three to four minutes. The rest of the kids hear how much fun we are having and can't wait to get to my table.

We would then go over homework. I would write down or mentally note who didn't turn it in.

See who struggled with it, address it later. Maybe take a minute here.

So now we had about twenty minutes to work on Writing, go over the Reading Anthology chapter test, and dictation sentences with the week's sight words. Quick assessment. "Jimmy, give me your eight-fact family." Make notes. Whatever you think needs to be hit on in a smaller setting. Usually, after the second rotation got to me, we would look at what they had done at the previous stations. Some serious learning goes on here. But the primary focus at my station was to provide individual help with their current writing assignments.

This station is designed to have enough independent work (usually their writing projects) to allow me to jump up and float the room for a few minutes. All of the other stations had specific menus. My table was more spontaneous. This is where connections are really made. This is where you get to know the academic strengths and weaknesses of your kids that not only helps you plan appropriate lesson plans but gives you the ammunition you need to 'Be the Expert' in your parent conferences. But most of all, this station allows everyone to get to know each other, to trust one another, and to care about each other.

You're building a family.

We would switch about every 25 minutes. Not etched in granite. If you go over five minutes, no big deal. Remember, it's your schedule! We usually started rotations at 9:00 and went up until lunch, 11:30. I would move kids around in my groups to see what worked best. If I did have a couple of groups who didn't work quite as fast as the others, I would not put them back-to-back. Like I said earlier, our morning pacing was pretty rapid. At the end of one year, a mother told me that her daughter said that she felt like she had just been through two years of school, and she was smiling.

The next station was Spelling, the kids would have a menu of activities that focused on the week's spelling pattern. If you're not happy with your current spelling curriculum, visit Scientific Spelling on the world wide web. It's easy, logical, and the kids really succeed. Even the lows.

Highlighting the spelling pattern in each word, red and blue letters, dividing words into syllables, word searches, unscrambling the mixed-up words, generating new words with the same spelling pattern, and using the words in sentences. Attack those words! I told my kids, "Bricks build walls. Words build sentences. Sentences build paragraphs and paragraphs build stories." If you are a master word crafter, you will be a successful communicator. And those people who can communicate their feelings and ideas are the people who can do anything they want to do with their lives. You can probably tell that Spelling is important to me.

We would move on to the Math station. Again, we reinforced and extended the week's concepts. Always reviewing previous concepts to make sure they got it.

The menu would have various activities, starting with a review. Then gradually getting a bit more difficult. I would always include a few word problems to complement the computations. Mix it up. Throw in some time and money activities. And kids love and need to practice measuring things. It can be as simple as measuring the length and width of your textbook. Later, ask, "Find the area and perimeter." Later in the school year, we would practice a couple of standardized word problems.

(After we had taught the skills in class). The Math station is also a great place to have the kids get on a computer and utilize some of the fantastic programs that are out there. And when you have a Math center, you're teaching Math twice a day two times a week. That's a good thing.

After another 25 minutes, switch to Reading. Some teachers would ask me how I signal my kids to switch stations. Some teachers would use a series of two bells or soft music. I tried several different ways, but it just wasn't me. We did focus on telling time, so the kids knew to be aware of the clock. I might say, watch the time. We started at 9:15. If we're working 25 minutes, what time will we switch? Hopefully, someone would answer correctly. In every class, there were always a few kids who were on the ball. It was never a major problem. More times than not, I would just yell, "Switch!"

I tried to make the Reading Station focus on not just learning, but enjoyment. The kids might reread the weekly story out of our Anthology series. Depending on the time of the year, we might have a short reading selection that focused on our test-taking skills. The kids would always bring this to my table so we could go over it together (Immediate feedback-more later).

I would provide Kids National Geographics, maps, and restaurant menus. They might have time to read their library books. And sometimes we would read our Science and Social Studies textbooks. These are typically a year ahead of the grade level for some reason. We need to focus more on non-fiction in Elementary. I'm not a big fan of partner-reading. I rarely saw the benefits. I would use my table to address that.

This might be a good place to incorporate a Technology station. The kids could work on actual computer skills and visit your favorite Math and Language Arts programs. It could be a stand-alone station or you could have the other stations absorb what you wanted them to work on. Yes, I know. A self-contained Elementary classroom is Heaven.

I always wanted the Writing Station to come right before the students came to me. That way I could look over their work quickly and gauge where each one was in the process. There was a menu here, too. Depending on the grade level, you could have a few minutes of Handwriting practice. But the main focus here is Writing. We want to utilize our word attack skills and our sentence-building skills and our increased vocabulary (sight-words) as we write. We always had two writing projects going. The short one was called Paragraph Building. It started on Monday and was finished on Friday. A completed final copy. The second project was usually a non-fiction piece that went through the entire writing process. I used a form of Six Traits of Writing by Ruth Culham. All of the stations are important, but this station is where everything seemed to come together.

I actually looked forward to each new group coming to see me. Someone usually brought me a Ding Dong or a Twinkie or a Ho Ho.

I'm not going to lie to you. Putting a successful rotation program together is not easy. It takes time and effort. A lot of effort.

So, ease into it. Take a little time to lay down the foundation of how your classroom is going to work. Teach them about menus. Post the daily schedule. "If you can read the schedule and menu, you will be successful." Post your weekly spelling words and sight words on the wall where they will be each week for the next 35 weeks. Stability. Routine. Tell them what a Monday will look like. Then Tuesday, Wednesday, Thursday, and Friday.

Each morning after Announcements, tell them what they will be doing from 8:00 right up until dismissal. And use a calm, confident voice. Not too fast and not too slow. When I started teaching, I talked so fast that I actually made myself slow down by pausing and counting 1, 2, 3 in my head. Breathe, count, begin again. After you have gone over the schedule, ask questions: "So, Jimmy, what are we doing first?"

"Sally, what time is snack time?" Take enough time to build the foundation. It will pay off.

After a week or two of traditional direct teach, guided practice, and independent practice, say to your class, "Hey, next week we are going to add something new." Introduce rotations. Explain what they are, how they work, and most importantly, why you are going to do it.

Start with one day, maybe Wednesdays. After morning announcements, bring out the rotation menu and explain it exactly the way you explained your daily schedule. Show them what it looks like. Demonstrate each station, how to switch, voice levels, restroom breaks, eating snacks during rotations, where to find the materials they will need, and where to turn in their assignments (One basket for completed, one basket for unfinished).

Take the whole day the first time you try it. Then you won't feel rushed. Take mental notes throughout the day. What worked? What didn't? What was absolutely awful? At what time did you feel really good? (Not dismissal) Make adjustments. Successful and fun rotations don't happen overnight. It is a living organism and will develop and grow as you go. The next time you try it, cut the time. Instead of the whole day, try to speed it up. Make your goal to be finished by lunch. And if you aren't, no big deal. Go to lunch, come back, and start right in. "OK class, go to the last station you were in before we went to lunch." Remember, it's your schedule. Work it!

Some classes will get it a lot faster than other classes. You know every year is different. Keep going. Two days a week. The weeks will pass. Your kids will get better. They will settle in, and start looking forward to Tuesdays and Wednesdays. I have had kids come into the room first thing in the morning and ask, "Are we doing rotations today?"

They seemed disappointed when I said, "Not today." The best part is that you will get better. More confident. Your pacing will get better. Your comfort level will grow. And you will discover that when you do a regular whole group direct teach, you even do that better than before. Your kids will be more accountable, and they will treat each other better.

Once you get your feet wet, work out some of the kinks and feel pretty confident about what you're doing, add some parents! Ask the ones who helped you put up supplies on the first day of school. Use those connections to build a Family in your classroom. It won't take long for these parents to start spreading the news and start recruiting other parents. I know, I know. Most teachers are scared to death to have parents watch them teach. But you are not 'most teachers.' At first, ask one parent to help, and train them to run a station exactly like you do. Then cross-train them to be able to work all of the stations. Later, they can train new parents.

Rule Number 1: Do not change your style of teaching because a parent is in the room. Be yourself. That is the whole point. Let them get to know you and see for themselves what 'great learning' is going on in their child's classroom. They will witness firsthand your passion, dedication, and love for your classroom Family. Believe me, they will spread the news throughout the community. And you will have a friend and supporter for life.

By showing your true self, the parents in your classroom will see you as 'one of them.' You are breaking down that wall of uncertainty and mistrust that is killing our schools. Remember the Triangle of Education? By having parents be a part of your plan, and actually helping teach their own kids, you are building the baselines of the entire Triangle. Your classroom will become a place that your students want to be, a place where parents want to be. But the best part, it will be a place where YOU WANT TO BE.

Running a self-contained classroom that includes two days of rotations works better than what is going on in most American classrooms today. I realize that we are going through incredibly difficult times, but at some point, we are going to have to try something different. Going back to the status quo is certainly not the answer. I know there will be significant changes when we return to a sense of normality. We need to seize this opportunity. Having Elementary classrooms that build connections between Student, Teacher, and Parent would allow us to lay that Foundation of Trust. The sense of Family that makes us all strong. When you implement these types of strategies, you can actually feel the Triangle growing.

Just a thought: Daily Rewards increase exponentially when you add rotations to your schedule. So do snacks.

Chapter Sixteen: Grading Papers: How, Where and When

Grades are necessary for everyone in the Triangle. Parents need to know how their kids are doing. Teachers need them in order to plan meaningful lesson plans, and Students need to know that their efforts are paying off. They need to know where they might need some help, but they especially need to know where they are doing great. Celebrate that. Grades need to accurately reflect the individual student's knowledge and skills. When your grades do this, it's another way of becoming the 'Expert in the Room.'

I can remember sitting in the teachers' lounge on a Wednesday before the Friday that grades were due for that period and hearing "Man, I need to get my grades in." Then another teacher would say, "I need to get some grades."

I have known teachers that would grade papers daily and weekly, but then would leave stacks of the graded papers on their desks until that very last week. I'm talking stacks a foot tall. "I just have to put them in the book."

"Just?" The word 'just' does not work here. Can you imagine a kid knocking them over by accident? I would JUST walk out the door and head for the nearest bar.

It's like being in college. If you keep up with the daily reading assignments, you're going to be OK. Put your grades in as soon as you grade the assignment. You'll be able to see your own kids over the weekend (Unless you don't want to see your own kids).

I tried to provide immediate feedback for most of my assessments. It does no one any good to give a quiz back a week later. And to get that authentic grade for the six week or nine-week period, you have to give your students enough opportunities to show what they know. Remember, this is Elementary school. It's not college where you might have a couple of projects, a mid-term, and a final. And the more grades you have (within reason), the easier it is to defend in those lovely parent conferences.

"How come Jimmy has a 78 in Math? I know he's smarter than that." Have your print-out ready (5 Ps) and say, "Well, I took 35 grades during that nine-week period, ranging from daily work that I helped the students with, quizzes, to chapter and unit tests." If you want to, tell them that you even threw out Jimmy's two lowest grades because Elementary kids are still young and don't feel great every day.

"So. Mr. Smith, Jimmy had 33 opportunities to demonstrate his math skill set."

Don't stop talking. Don't open the window. Calmly and without judgment, continue explaining. "Based on his grades, I do know what his areas of concern are." Tell his dad what your plan is, how rotations work, when you are available to work with him during your day (before school), and what they can do at home.

Remind the parents that you do send homework and graded papers home each week with Jimmy and that you have sent progress reports home (School District Policy).

Then shut up, sit back, and wait for a response. Then, this usually works, "I love Jimmy." We have talked about this; he knows where he needs to put the work in. Let's continue what we are doing. I will work with him more during rotations. Let's give it three weeks and see where we are. Then I will e-mail you every Friday and keep you updated.

You have taken control. Answered his question professionally and laid out a plan of action. That's all you can do. Unless…you have something personal you can add.

I always throw in this story. "I have two boys. One is fantastic in Math. His High School teacher actually asks him to check her work. The other one does great in Language Arts. He gets 100s on all of his spelling tests and actually competed in the third-grade spelling bee when he was in the second grade. But he doesn't do well in Math. If my one son brings home a 98 in Math on his report card, I ask him."

"What's the deal?" When my other son brought home a 73 in Math, we would go out to eat to celebrate. Because I knew he was doing the best he could. Humanize. Parents don't come in that often. When they do, take advantage of the opportunity. Break down the wall. Briefly explain how you teach Math and suggest they come in to help or just watch.

"We have several parents who help with rotations. The kids love it." And have a big poster of the Power of a Triangle clearly visible.

We all know how to grade, but what we grade and when we grade are just as important. We did use Fridays to assess basic stuff. But we worked up to that Friday testing with a well-planned routine of instruction and activities. If I felt we weren't ready, we would wait until Tuesday or Wednesday of the following week. Never tested on Mondays. Didn't seem fair to Elementary age kids.

Math is the easiest to grade. A lot of computations, and answers that don't require interpretation. However, most chapter and unit tests have a lot of word problems.

And don't get me started on standardized Math tests. They are essentially Reading tests. We would do some kind of written daily work in Math. I would usually take a grade two to three times during the week. Another advantage of being self-contained is that you know what your kids know (And don't know) This is where the quickies come in. Plan ahead. Know when Library time is. Know who and what you're testing before you go. Grab two to three kids each visit for one minute's quizzes. Silent reading time offers five more opportunities each week. Squeeze every minute. Remember, you have pre-planned these. You know exactly what you're looking for. It's quick. And you can use your Math rotation for an occasional quiz. Add reviews, chapter and unit tests and you won't have any problems collecting enough authentic grades for your six- or nine-week period.

During Chat Time a student came up to me and asked, "Mr. Teel, my mom wants to know what I can do to bring my Math grade up."

"Quit missing so many." I answered. Later that week, we implemented a new Friday assessment named in honor of the girl who asked the question. It consisted of ten basic review computations (With a heavy emphasis on basic). It was designed to be taken after the regular Friday quiz to help all students raise their grades. I told my class that it was indeed named after the young lady, and for the rest of my teaching career, we would do it every Friday. The kids would take it while I started grading the regular quiz. It really did help raise grades a little, except for the one who the review was named for.

I wanted every assessment tool I used to be an accurate measure of my students' knowledge and skills. I used tests and quizzes tied directly to our curriculum as well as teacher-created materials. Mostly my own. I didn't do anything ground-breaking, just logical assessments based on what we covered to give me accurate data. I found that self-designed quizzes and tests were easier and quicker to grade. I never used a key. Believe it or not, there are errors in the giant curriculum companies' material that our school districts purchase. In Reading, we would read the weekly story from our anthology. We would mix it up depending on what time of the school year it was. I would always do a Read-a-Loud for the first reading. Kids need to hear what fluency sounds like. Sometimes we would take turns reading paragraphs (That tied into our paragraph building) Later in the year, the kids would read it a second time and take it home one night a week to read with their parents. To make sure they got it, we would fill out a story map on Thursdays. It was just a piece of copy paper with the title and who, when, where, problem, solution, and three major events as headers. Each section was worth a certain amount of points. Problem and Solution were worth the majority. We did the first ones together. Then gradually turn them loose to do it on their own. We would grade it together right before we took the quiz provided by the anthology series. It helped immensely with comprehension and yes, two weekly grades! I always took the weekly story quiz at the same time the class would. I want to know what they know. These quizzes were made up of ten multiple-choice questions. Two answers bordered on ridiculous. We would laugh at them later as we graded them, but two of the answers were fairly similar. One week I graded the quiz earlier and passed them out to the kids. Later in the day a student came up to my table and questioned why I marked one of his answers wrong. We looked at it together, and I explained how I came up with a different answer choice. He had his book with him. He opened it up to the page and said that it says in the second paragraph what was clearly a logical answer to the question. I looked at it and told him that I agreed. We then discussed how both answers worked. He had proven his point, but more importantly, he had the confidence to come to my table. Later in the day, I shared the story with the whole class. I told them that I'm not always right just because I'm the teacher. If you don't agree with something, say something.

Every year our class read four-chapter books. Our school district supplied us with a list of recommended titles based on grade level. I'm sure every district in the country does this. We treated it as a read-a-loud and covered just two chapters a day. I usually read right after silent Reading Time or if our schedule was tight, replacing SSR. Before I started to read, we would go over the two questions per chapter that I had written on the board (two concrete and two abstract).

Sometimes, we would answer the questions whole group right after reading. Sometimes the kids would complete the questions and turn them in. But I always took at least two grades per week on the chapter book questions.

Individual Reading Inventories are excellent assessment tools. They provide useful data, show progress, and are easy to grade. I would administer three per student every semester. More often if the student was struggling, maybe not as often for your fluent readers. An IRI is an accurate measure of a student's reading ability and is easy to explain to parents. A terrific addition to a student's portfolio. And when you go over one in a conference, it clearly demonstrates who the 'Expert in the Room' is. Again, plan ahead, use your SSR time, Library time, whenever you can squeeze your schedule.

One other quick, effective assessment is to have a student come to your table and read a paragraph. Look for fluency, words per minute, self-correcting, and say, "Tell me in one sentence. What's the gist?" Of course, you take a few notes, assign a grade. Done.

Don't freak out about Writing grades. Let the Language/Arts portion carry the weight. One weekly spelling test, two to three grammar grades a week. We used our weekly sight words for dictation sentences. Easy grading. Actual writing grades are a bit more difficult. They take more time. We did a Paragraph Build every week. It helps reinforce parts of speech, sentence structure, and dialogue. We started with a topic sentence on Monday. Then added a specific type of sentence each week. By Friday, the kids had written, edited, and completed a final copy. You could end it there, or have the kids add to it the following week. There's a grade. At the same time, everyone would be working on a Six Traits writing assignment. The whole process usually took two weeks. We used My Table during Rotations to conference, and this is what we used when kids were finished with their other work. They could always pull their sloppy copy out and work on it while everyone else was finishing up. The kids would come up to me and say, "Mr. Teel, what do I do now."

After I replied, "Have you finished your writing?" a few times, they wouldn't even ask. I would watch them walk over to the file cabinet and pull out their writing. Some teachers and most parents want to know how you grade writing. We had specific standards for Paragraph Building, and I used the Six Traits rubric and conversion chart for the longer assignments.

When I graded the longer assignments, I would write on the student's paper the number for each trait according to the rubric (we had taught what each trait was). Then convert it to a numerical grade. To make sure I had the grades right, I would sit on the floor and put the papers in ascending order. Take the first paper, then the next one. Was it better or not as good? Keep adding all of the writing assignments until you have put them all in one line across the floor. The best one is on the far right. The worst one is on the far left. The middle paper is probably going to turn out to be a C unless you have an entire class of fantastic writers. I guess it could go the other way. Ouch.

The grade is important to your kids, but the comments on the back is where you can reach and teach your kids to write. Take the time to write specific suggestions. Move this sentence. Find a synonym for this word. Maybe use dialogue to tell this part. It needs a supporting detail here. And celebrate the good stuff. Don't just write, love it or great job! Tell them what part works and why. Yes, this takes time, but you are teaching here. This is where great writing starts!

Without a doubt, the worst part of teaching Elementary kids how to write is when you introduce Dialogue. Why do they love it so? I had a student who could and would write four pages of nothing but dialogue. And absolutely no she saids or he saids. None. Every time I came across her paper, I would put it at the bottom of the pile. I had to be in the perfect mindset to tackle it. No, not drunk. On Monday, while I was passing out the graded papers, she would say, "Mr. Teel. I didn't get my paper back." After dodging the real reason, I finally confessed that her writing was so much more sophisticated that I had to have the perfect conditions to properly grade it. No one could be home. No TV or music playing in the house, and the lights had to be dimmed. Even my dog had to stay outside.

By the end of the year, she was a pretty good writer. 'Nice use of dialogue.'

Social Studies and Science are totally different animals when it comes to grades. You don't need as many as Math and Language/Arts, and you really don't have the time to generate many. I would get a head start in SS by using a daily geography lesson by Evan-Moor. We used it as a warm-up to start the SS lesson. Sometimes we included it in our Rotations. The DGL focuses on basic map skills and introduces kids to that big world out there. We would go over it quickly each day, then turn it in on Friday. I took a quiz grade on the five-day package. At the start of each new chapter in our textbook, we would start a reverse book walk. It's an excellent way to learn the material while you're teaching your kids how to read non-fiction. The students would turn them in when we completed the chapter. Quizzes, chapter reviews, chapter and unit tests are other things you can grade. We tried to do a writing project each grading period. It might be a short research paper on a famous person in history or a foreign country (There's a Social Studies and a Writing grade!)

I treated Science the same way. In addition to the textbook, we had a couple of computer programs with short videos on everything from the scientific method to the planets. They also provided quizzes. We did a few actual group lab experiments. Then had the kids do a write-up. The number of labs we did depended on the maturity of the class. Usually, we went to whole group demonstrations. The class would present a hypothesis, discuss the results and determine if it was proved or not. We used the reverse book walk with the textbook. Chapter reviews, tests, and unit tests provided enough opportunities to assess what the kids knew. We also incorporated writing projects that dealt with science concepts. Our classroom library shelves were filled with short easy-to-read biographies of famous inventors that we used for book reports. Be creative. Work in an annual class science fair. Just make sure your assessments give an accurate reflection of what the kids know. I had a student one year who would bomb every Science chapter test we took. I would sit with him at my table and ask him the same questions orally or just say, "Hey, what is a hypothesis?" or "What are the three types of heat transfer?" He knew more about it than I did.

School districts differ on how they handle homework. Some grade it, some don't.

It's not that you grade it that makes it important. Homework serves a purpose. That is well-thought-out and relevant homework. It should be designed to match what you did in class that day or what you covered quite recently. My son would bring home a homework packet designed for the whole month and you were allowed to do it anytime, just as long as you turned it in by the end of the month. Well, I helped my kids throughout their school years. But, it didn't make any sense for my son to ask me to help him with a concept he hadn't seen before. Frustrating and upsetting kids is not the purpose of homework. I know. I know. Parents are really busy with soccer and music lessons, etc. But I don't want my kids spending three hours on the first Monday night of the month wrestling with homework.

It should take ten to fifteen minutes to reinforce the concept that is still in the kid's head. If it takes longer than that, stop. Write me a note and I will address the problem that very next day.

I gave homework for two reasons: to reinforce what we did in class, and to develop organization and accountability. To be clear, homework time is separate from nightly reading time.

We had a policy regarding homework. It was due when the morning bell rang. The kids would drop it off in the homework basket as part of the morning routine. I did not accept it after the bell. No exceptions. Well, maybe one.

I was sitting at my Reading table listening to morning announcements when he came in. He started walking toward me as I thought, *Late, again.* He was doing everything right. Putting away his backpack, grabbing a pencil, and dropping his homework in the basket.

As he stood there, I picked up his paper and asked, "What's this?"

"Homework."

"This is yesterday's."

He started to walk back to his desk as I crumpled his homework into a ball, and gently tossed it over my shoulder in the direction of the wastebasket. The paper ball rebounded off the wall right into the basket. Score! He must have heard the crumpling of his hard work and turned around. Realizing what had happened, his whole demeanor changed. His eyes bulged. His body stiffened. I must admit, I had never seen this side of him. He wasn't even looking at me. His stare was focused on the trash can. Out of nowhere, he charged in my direction, not like a bull, but more like a duck violently flapping its wings. I am not making the rest of this up. The young man dove forward, sliding on the floor under my little table, crashing headfirst into the trash can. He stood up and began feverishly rummaging through the discarded paper until he came upon the crumpled homework. As he picked it up, he lost his balance and fell backward into the brown metal can. He was just big enough to be seated with both his arms and legs dangling from the can, but small enough to not be able to move. He was stuck. He looked like a turtle laying on its back in the middle of the road. But he was holding the sought-after homework in his right hand.

After not completely grasping what I had just seen, I stood up, took one step, and looked down at the struggling turtle. I offered my hand. He took it. Together we worked him out of the wastebasket. He stood there, gathering himself. We looked at each other for a second.

"OK, I'll take it."

"Thank you, Mr. Teel."

I smoothed out his homework nice and flat and put it in the homework basket. He walked back to his desk. I'm certain he was smiling. I was.

That incident cemented our connection and did more than provide a Daily Reward.

That was a Lifetime Reward.

Chapter Seventeen: Before and After

The whole point of this book is to show how important connections are and to use whatever time you have during the school day to make them happen. I didn't plan for these parts of my day to bring such amazing results. It all just evolved.

I used to get to school pretty early. I liked to do my morning stretches, make sure I had all the materials we were going to use for the day, check the room, put the word wall back up, make sure I had all the menus posted, and write the morning heading on the whiteboard. Just tighten up the plan for the day. When the kids walked in the door, I knew I was ready. When it felt right, I opened my door. I know a lot of parents have to get to work early, too. The kids who were dropped off would usually go straight to the cafeteria for breakfast. Some of the really early kids would stand outside and wait. Not a good practice, but it's a fact of life. I'm not sure when it started, but some of those kids who were in my class would walk past our door on the way to the cafeteria. I don't even remember who that first group of kids were. One morning a couple of my kids decided to walk in, say.

"Hi," and ask if they could stay in the room.

I was ready for the day so I said, 'Sure.'

Well, that opened the floodgate. A couple more would show up. Then the kids with younger siblings started to come and before you know it, former students.

And even kids who weren't in my class.

We did have parameters. Most of the kids finished their homework or pulled out their library books. Some would sit on the rug in our class library and read. It was the neatest thing to see kids in my class reading to their younger brother or sister. And watching my kids take them around the room, showing and explaining what all the menus meant. You could feel their pride. One year I had the best older sister ever. First, she would take her little sister to the cafeteria for breakfast. Then come down to our room, pick out a book, and share a quiet reading experience together. Almost every morning. I usually sat at my reading table. Soon, all the seats around it would be filled. Conversations ranged from what they watched on TV the night before to what we were going to do that day. Sometimes I would help with homework. There were doughnuts. But mostly, I would let the kids talk. Just sit back. Listen.

That twenty to thirty minutes was a goldmine. It provided an opportunity to strengthen existing connections and even start new ones. The kids who walked into that open classroom who were a grade level below got a glimpse of what they could expect next year. They saw what our Family looked like.

And when kids want to be in the classroom when they don't have to be, you're doing something right. You are providing something those kids need. One of my goals was to have the kids actually want to show up every morning. Well, these kids were showing up early.

After school was an entirely different animal. It was the end of an almost always energy-packed day. Everyone was a bit tired. Definitely a lower-key atmosphere than the before-school time. We used the after-school time to wrap up, clean a bit, and tutor.

Each day our class started a basic cleaning of the room about 15 minutes before the bell. It was a pretty basic cleaning. We would do the heavy stuff later. I did what most teachers do: post the jobs and weekly assignments on the board. Organize the trash, collect the pencils (Not sharpen them, too loud), put the chairs up in three or four stacks, not on the desks, sweep the floor. Basic.

After either car or bus duty, I would grab another sweet tea and head for my room. I tutored most days. Those kids would come in, take a seat, and have snack time while I organized all of the written work the class had produced during the day. If it was a rotation day, I would just grab the papers in the baskets and toss them in my bag. I would go through them at home and decide which ones to grade. A lot of the work was already graded. The work that I had already 'speed graded' during the day was in a stack next to my computer. If there was enough time, I would go ahead and enter them.

There are quite a few teachers' kids in Elementary schools. They seem to congregate in the hallways after the day is done. Once again, these kids saw an open door and asked if they could come in. Some of them were in my class, others weren't.

I said, "Sure, but when I have tutees, you need to be quiet." Well, they would come in, eat a snack, and usually do their homework, or read. Sometimes, they would join us at my table for the routine card warm-up. One day when there weren't any tutees, I suggested that we clean the room. I told them that I worked as a school custodian to make it through college, and it was hard work. We were a big school and did not have that many custodians.

"Let's help." That was the start of our student daily cleaning crew. It was a core of three to five teacher kids who did an amazing job. Dusting, wiping desks, some serious floor-sweeping, and even pencil sharpening. But they had to take the Ticonderogas to another room (Too loud) I don't know why, but having a squeaky-clean whiteboard was my number one priority. For 18 years! Well, my expectations became theirs. When they were done, the room looked fantastic!

That year the administration started a 'Golden Trash Can Award.' The second shift custodians would decide which room in the school was the cleanest each day and leave the coveted can outside of the winning room. No contest. Our class was clearly the cleanest because of our professional cleaning team (Yes, I did pay them for their services. I always tried to connect education to the 'real world.') After a few weeks, one of the custodians confided in me. She admitted that if it were up to her, my class would win every day. But, it wasn't, she was told to spread the gold can around for school morale.

I have to admit. I was lucky. My family supported me when I went in a little early and stayed a little late. School was important to all of us. With that extra time, I was able to solidify the connections we made during the day. The extra time allowed for even more Daily Rewards.

I don't know how or who came up with the name for our afternoon cleaning crew. Anyway, we started to refer to ourselves as the Fighting Nancies. Yes, I helped clean. And, I know, I know, I know. Not politically correct! But we were a proud group and we took our name seriously. I remember one afternoon I stepped out for a bit. When I returned, I heard someone shouting. I was curious so I waited just outside the door and listened to the leader of the crew.

"You call yourself a fighting Nancy? Get the board clean before Mr. Teel gets back."

Shared expectations make for a smooth day. A smooth year.

That was a fantastic group of teachers' kids. They all took pride in their school work and always carried themselves with class and style. I hope someday they are able to read this chapter, and know just how proud I was of them, then and even now.

Powerful connections:

Every morning I would write the morning heading on the whiteboard. Such as:

Today is Friday, January 19, 2008.
Lineleader: Jesus
Helper: Christian

Well, throughout the day, kids would come up to the front of the room for different reasons. Sometimes rubbing against the board. We tried to maintain the message, and keep it looking good. But apparently one day we didn't keep it updated. My assistant principal came in one afternoon, visited a bit, looked at the whiteboard, and said, "Man, you've got clout." I looked at what she was pointing to.

Today is Friday, January 19, 2008.
Lineleader: Jesus
         Christ

Chapter Eighteen: Teaching to the Test (It's Safe and Effective!)

"Mr. Teel, last night at dinner my brother said that his teacher told him the STAAR test is the most important day in his life."

"Well, let's see. The most important day in your life. Wow! Well, there's your wedding. And you'll probably get married a couple of times. Jimmy, I'm guessing three." Laughter filled the classroom.

Change the setting to the teacher workroom. "I am so tired of teaching to this stupid test. We could be doing so much more." "I didn't comment." But in my head, I was thinking, "That's what we do each and every day." Every time you teach a math concept, you're teaching to the test. Every time you teach main idea or supporting details, you're teaching to the test. Because your kids will use everything you have taught them on the test!

I only taught in Texas. Other states may do things differently. But the Lone Star State lays out exactly what each grade level is supposed to cover over the course of the school year. It's pretty specific. I never had any confusion about what my responsibilities were. The flawed theory being if you cover the TEKS, your students will be prepared for the test. The test is not the problem. It's the school administration's unnecessary emphasis on that singular event. I know it's about money and district reputations and ultimately, jobs. I get it, but I also get that teaching is teaching. But there is another problem. The pressure on teachers is to not only teach the curriculum but at the same time, teach their students the test-taking skills that they will need their entire lives. Being in a well-run self-contained elementary setting gives the teacher the time to do both. And to do both well.

Every test and quiz I gave throughout the year was important. We treated them all the same. Are they? Of course not. Not academically. We all know chapter and unit tests carry more weight when it comes to grading. But if you use your daily schedule and 'Squeeze every minute,' your students will have the test-taking skills and more importantly, the confidence and emotional skills to do their best on that year-end standardized test.

I know what you're thinking. Who is this guy? He sounds like some early Sunday morning evangelist. Far from it. My classes took those year-end tests 18 times without any crying or sleepless nights. Some of my kids looked forward to them because they wouldn't have to listen to me for a day (That hurt) And we always ranked at or near the top of the district's results.

I never understood our administration's inability to handle the test. Did they think the results were going to be any different from the rest of the year's assessments? I never saw a solid reader do poorly on the Reading test and

I never saw a struggling reader do great. I suppose a kid could feel ill or have a fight with a parent thirty minutes before school. Life happens. But for the most part, the kids who don't pass usually are the kids who can't read (especially non-fiction) or don't have a good foundation in Math, or both. And because of the connections we built the previous nine months and the fact that we knew our kids inside and out, we had a pretty good idea of how things were going to go. I could predict with a high degree of accuracy how many questions each kid in my class was going to miss. In 18 years I never said, "Wow! I can't believe Jimmy got a 100!"

It's easy to say not to worry about it so much when the principal and some parents are stressing out. But your stress flows directly to your students. They feel it. So how do you get there? How do you get to the point where you are comfortable with the test and how your kids are going to perform?

Accept the fact that we are teaching to the test. Every test. That end-of-the-year standardized test is no different. It may look different, especially if you're testing online, but it won't when your kids get to it. That's where we come in. Don't separate it from any other assessment you give. Don't give it any extra importance. All tests and quizzes are important. I barely mentioned the test to my kids until later in the year. And I sure as hell didn't scare my parents with it on Meet the Teacher Night! I used to tell my classes that we use tests to see what you know and what you don't know. Then I can make my lesson plans. "Every test you guys take is a test of me." They knew that we were in this together. We shared the same goal. This is indeed a Family.

Remember all that stuff about being self-contained and how great rotations are? Well, if you want your kids to have all the tools to be successful on any test. If you want to reduce the stress levels for everyone involved, (including your own family at home), pour yourself another glass of wine, and read on. I am not encouraging drinking. I'm a realist.

It's all about time. The time you and your kids are together. We talked about making genuine connections with your students and their parents, and how those connections build a sense of family in your classroom. Because of that time spent together day after day, sticking to your daily schedule, doing rotations, and offering stability and consistency, you are developing trust. You are creating an environment that can't help but foster Learning. From the morning bell to dismissal, you and your kids are immersed in each other's lives. You will become an effective teacher. Someone who doesn't just deliver material, but a teacher who delivers material that makes its way in. Your students will be more receptive to what you're saying because they know you care about each and every one of them (Yes, even Jimmy). At the end of each year, I was amazed at the growth of my students. Not always academic growth, but emotional and social growth. The way they handled themselves and most importantly, the way they treated each other.

I always told my kids that they should walk into a room "like they owned the place." Not cocky, not rude, but confident. And knowledge is a big part of that. Be prepared. And if you are in an unfamiliar situation, ask questions, and listen. This is a major component of reducing the anxiety kids feel about tests.

Making 'testing' a normal part of life reduces kids' stress levels and you start doing that the first day of school. We really didn't address the end of the year stuff at all during the first semester. We covered what we were supposed to cover and we tested the kids to see what they knew. Not Earth-shattering. The type of assessment you start the year with obviously depends on what grade you're teaching. If your district's philosophy is K-5 self-contained, the fourth and fifth graders are 'old veterans.' They get it. Those upper-grade teachers are benefiting from the lower-grade teachers' family building.

We used weekly quizzes in spelling and grammar, but even there, we taught the kids how to take a spelling test. Listen to the word. Break the sounds apart. Then ask yourself, "What letters make those sounds?" Then put those letters together to make the word. Picture this week's list in your mind. See the black letters on the white background. It was neat to watch some of the kids look up to where the spelling list was posted each week. I remember one time I forgot to take the list down. A few of the kids pointed at it and smiled. I put my finger to my mouth and shook my head.

When the test was over, Jimmy said, "Mr. Teel, you forgot to take the spelling words down."

"Then why did you miss two?" Immediate feedback.

In Reading, we read the stories from our anthology. A ten question multiple-choice test was provided for each selection. This is a great place to start. It doesn't look like the standardized test, but it offers the chance to start attacking the questions, considering each answer response, and discussing why they are right, and why they are wrong.

"Prove it. Find that in the story." We went over each of those tests either as a whole group or as part of rotations. You can't just grade this, pass them out at the end of the week, and expect your kids to develop the strategies they need. Ain't gonna happen. We used the Science and Social Studies textbooks the same way. Although we usually did a reverse book walk before, we read each chapter.

Word problems are the main focus of those standardized Math tests. Kids have to be able to read well to succeed. They have to know what is this question asking me to do? Start with basic stuff (We even showed the kids how to get faster with mad minutes). Then add more complex strategies. Most math curriculums come with standard chapter and unit tests. Those will do. Some curriculums come with additional assessments that mimic the EOY tests. We used those in the second semester.

I was always amazed at how different the kids looked when they came back from Christmas break. Taller, more mature-looking. Even their faces looked a little different. I wonder if they saw the same thing when they looked at me. Definitely more mature looking.

I liked the second semester better. We had already laid the foundation, made some connections, started acting like a family. There seems to be fewer distractions in the Spring semester. The weather starts to warm up. I just felt better. Energized. Now we started thinking about that dreaded test.

Remember, we have been teaching to all tests since day one. But not in isolation. We are teaching the required curriculum and showing the kids how to take a test at the same time.

We are using those assessments to gauge how the kids are doing. Now it's time to develop those basic test-taking skills. The strategies that they need to be successful on the EOY tests and every test they take for the rest of their lives. And we are going to do it the same way we did in the first semester: teaching curriculum and more developed test-taking skills together. They are not mutually exclusive. You teach the more specific skills to deliver the subject matter and the actual problem-solving skills.

I'm not telling you anything you don't already know and do. But this is what we did year in and year out with really good results. I looked at my calendar to verify the actual test dates. Then I backtracked from that date. I decided what concepts to hit, what materials I was going to use, and how I was going to deliver the material. Where would I direct-teach? When would I use mini-lessons? And most importantly, how would I use my rotations to utilize time effectively? Of course, I went there. You knew I would. When you utilize rotations in a well-run self-contained Elementary classroom, 'Teaching to the Test' becomes manageable.

It's your schedule. You can 'squeeze every minute.' Your kids are more receptive. There are fewer behavior issues. It's a safe, comfortable environment where effective teaching happens.

And remember, you are teaching the required curriculum while you reinforce test-taking skills. And you are using those skills to actually teach the subject matter. It's not impossible to teach main idea, sequencing, or fact and opinion by using multiple-choice questions. We would pretend to be word detectives and attack the questions. The kids loved it!

There is a lot to cover in Reading, so I would decide on the concepts to hit based on what I knew about my class from the first semester. Topics ranged from main idea, sequencing, author's purpose, cause and effect, vocabulary, to supporting details. I usually backtracked twelve to fifteen weeks. Pretty much the whole Spring semester. Each week I would add the specific concept to what we were already doing that week in Reading. I wasn't really introducing anything new to the class. They already had experience with main idea and the other concepts. But I was showing them new ways to understand the concepts. Not in isolation, but by teaching test-taking skills that also reinforced the actual curriculum. We just added this new stuff to our weekly reading series and our chapter book read-a-louds. The point is, we didn't drop what we had been doing all year.

The next week, we would add a new concept, but always reviewing the previous week's concept. Then another and another. Every four weeks, I would give a reading selection quiz that covered the four concepts together. I would use selections that assessed the targeted concept. There are dozens of ancillary products out there that fit the bill (Check your teacher closet. You never know what you might find). We kept adding and reviewing until we were about four weeks away from the test date.

Kids need to know what something looks like. I would pull the previous year's STAAR test to use as a practice run through. And we would do it together. You can't throw a practice test on a kid's desk and go sit down. And you sure as hell can't do it again two weeks later and complain in the workroom "These kids just aren't getting it." We would go over the selection as a whole group. Read the selection out loud. Do a story map at the bottom of the story together. If they know who's the who, where's the where, main characters, three major events, the problem, and the solution before they get to the questions, they will be fine. Then attack the questions as word detectives. They had all the tools they needed: from sequencing to fact and opinion. They could find the answers in the text. Then we would do another selection, making sure everyone had a chance to participate. Total time. Maybe thirty minutes. Then I would say, "Alright. Do the last one on your own. Have fun." It was neat to see kids jumping right in, knowing they had the knowledge and skills they needed to do their best. In addition to learning the necessary test-taking skills, kids need to have the physical stamina to handle the test. A good way to do this is to break down the test into more manageable parts. We would read one selection, fill in a story map, then attack the questions, utilizing every strategy and trick we knew to pick the best answer. Then we would close our test books, put our pencils down, and relax a bit. Some would walk down the hall, get a drink, use the restroom, then slowly walk back to class. Others would walk back to the healthy snack station, eat some fruit, sip a little water, chill for five minutes. I would monitor each student's break time in order to keep things moving. Then when the time was right, the kids would jump back in, and repeat the process. We know all kids are not the same when it comes to learning and do not respond in the same way. After months of preparation and suggestions, there were still a few who thought they were in an Olympic sprint. I remember some years I would barely have enough time to sip my sweet tea and open my Twinkie, when one of the sprinters would be standing at my little table, holding their completed end of the year State of Texas STAAR test. These kids were almost always girls. And they almost always had perfect scores. One of my sons was a fantastic hitter in baseball. His stance was not picture perfect. He could have spread his feet apart a bit more. Maybe bend his knees. He always made contact. I never tried to 'fix' him. Just saying.

We handled the Math test pretty much the same way. We laid down a good foundation of basic operations, combining both accuracy and a bit of speed. Backtracked from the test date and reviewed all the concepts: Measurement, money, time, geometry, patterns, etc. but we spent most of our time attacking word problems. Word problems that covered each and every category. During the year our class did a Math warm-up each day. Always right after Silent Reading Time. Sometimes for the daily morning warm-up, we included something like it in our Math rotation. So the kids were used to Math warm-ups. To break up the EOY Math test into manageable parts I suggested that the kids treat the whole test as a Math warm-up. Answer ten questions, close the test, put down the pencil, and break just like the Reading test. Pretend that was Monday. Now, go back to your desk and do Tuesday's warm-up. Break.

Wednesday. Before you know it, you have finished the week's math warm-ups. Once again, kids need to know how something works, so we did practice this technique during the second semester.

OK. Back to preaching. The easiest EOY Math test of my 18 years was the fourth grade class that I looped with from third grade. It was like taking a chapter test on a regular day of the week. Lots of Olympic sprinters that year. And most of them were gold medal winners. Easy breezy.

In Texas, fourth graders had to take an additional test. The Writing test. It included a little grammar and editing portion and a writing component. We had used the Six Traits (love it) and combined it with weekly Paragraph Building all year, so the kids knew how to combine the two. Quality with speed! They knew how to write an organized paragraph with a good opening, a few supporting details, and a bridge sentence to get the reader to the next paragraph. String three of those together, write a good closing so the reader knows it's over. Throw in a little dialogue and Bada Bing, Bada Boom, you're done.

I have not been in the classroom for a while. I realize that some states have adopted online EOY testing. But teachers are still teaching kids how to read and write. I'm pretty sure that math concepts are still being taught in American classrooms. Connections are being made and families are being built. I see this as another component added to the teacher's day. But you don't need to ask anyone how in the world am I going to fit this into my schedule?

You already know.

Chapter Nineteen: Classroom Management (It Takes More Than an Einstein)

I don't know if my students learned anything on my first day of teaching, but I sure did. It doesn't matter how much you know about Science or Math. And you can be the best writer on the face of the earth. But if you don't have great classroom management skills, you will not succeed. It's that simple.

Don't get me wrong. The more you know about the subject matter, the better. It's actually a good thing if you're somewhat of an expert. But that's all meaningless if the kids aren't listening. They have to buy what you're selling. You have to show them that all this stuff you're throwing at them will actually make an impact on their lives. A positive impact.

I remember my first week of being thrown into the fire (First grade) The word, 'survive' crossed my mind quite a few times each day. I had to break the day into sections just to make it. Morning bell to Camp. Camp to Lunch. Lunch to dismissal. You talk about a clock watcher! On my drive home, I would assess the day and either score it a win for them or for me. I remember saying, "Alright. I won that one." That was the first week of October.

It takes time. Not all teachers are the same. But after 18 years, I'm convinced most kids are. They're looking for guidance. Most young kids are looking for safe boundaries. They want to know what is expected of them. They want to know how all this stuff they hear each day is going to matter. They want someone to care and they want to belong. And they don't want surprises. When a classroom environment is built upon stability, consistency, and fairness, everything else starts falling into place.

Good classroom behavior doesn't happen overnight. It not only takes time, it takes effort. Day in and day out. You can't take a day off. Especially early in the school year. I'm not talking physically. You will need a day off every now and then, but your standards and expectations can't take a day off. If you line up a certain way and walk down the hall a certain way, that has to happen the same way every time you do it. That's right. Every *#@! time. I always explained to my kids why we are being quiet in the hallway. It's not just for the heck of it. Some classes might be taking a quiz. Relate it to their lives. "Don't you hate it when you're watching something and your little brother comes in the room and starts talking?"

"How rude!" Or you're trying to take a nap and somebody turns on the TV? It's called being aware of other people. It's called being nice.

Kids will behave better when they not only understand that their actions affect other people but actually care about other people. My mother used to say, "Never eat the last cookie." Leave it for the next person or offer to share it. It's a great way to teach kids that the world doesn't revolve around them. There is one drawback. I don't know how many times I threw away that one stale cookie.

Classroom behavior will improve when your students know and understand your daily classroom procedures. How to come into the room, how to get a new pencil, restroom breaks, 'Chat Time,' how to line up. All of it. You have to teach it. The kids need to see what it looks like and what it sounds like. I knew a teacher who recorded her class during Silent Reading Time. Then she played it for her class. It sounded like a prison riot. The kids listened to it, realized that it wasn't exactly 'silent' and got better. My teacher friend also explained to the kids why Silent Reading Time was important to her, and how it could have a positive effect on them. Kids listen, especially when a teacher takes a minute to make it personally meaningful.

Every year is different. Classroom dynamics and all that. I would guess that about a third of the kids would get it and climb on board. But it's the rest of the class that has to buy-in. It takes time. And that time has to be used correctly. Developing connections and building that classroom Family has to be a daily process. And you can't force it. It has to be real.

This all starts on the first day of school. Remember the 5 Ps. "Prior Planning Prevents Poor Performance." You've got your room ready. Your lesson plans are ready. And you have all the materials your kids are going to need for the week. Make that your Mantra. You will be ready every morning you walk into your classroom.

Modeling what you expect the behavior to be in your classroom is more important than talking about it. Yes, you will be explaining a lot those first few weeks, but don't preach. Try to demonstrate. Mix it up. Teach a little. Introduce the week's spelling words. Then show them how to get a pencil. Have fun. Be silly…but firm. Two things we stressed throughout the school year were 'Know your audience' and 'There's a time and a place.' If you're trying to instill stability and consistency, then you have to be the poster child. After a short introductory period, your kids will know exactly what your response will be in any situation that comes up. I remember when a student from another class walked in and interrupted our lesson. Every one of my kids gasped and looked my way. Waiting for the response they all knew was coming (Another teachable moment). It did.

We talked about how important it is to get to know your kids. Well, let them get to know you (Student to Teacher connection) I talked about my family all the time (Humanize) I bragged about my kids and told them what a great mom my 'Honey Bunny' was. When K-State beat Texas in football, I posted the newspaper article on the classroom door. We talked about General Hospital during Snack time. I even told my kids when I didn't feel well. And I would really appreciate it if they would bring it down a little that day. I lost my voice for about a week each and every year. I didn't feel bad, but all I could manage was a soft whisper. It was my favorite week of the year! I carried several flashcards around to get my point across. Some for my class: Yes, no, maybe, no recess for you! Some for my co-workers: Are those new shoes? Have you lost weight? We made it work. The kids were great. They would actually whisper back to me. What a wonderful, quiet week. It was almost like they cared about me.

It is not the purpose of this chapter to list specific classroom rules. You guys don't need that. Just about any practical list will be effective in a classroom where the kids feel safe and comfortable. They will understand not only what you are trying to accomplish in the classroom but why. Your students will see the effort you make to build genuine connections. Kids get it.

Every kid needs to know what you expect from them. And after being a part of the Family within your classroom, those expectations become the norm. I can't stress enough how easy my year was when we looped from third to fourth. Hands down. Best year ever.

But I do have a few general suggestions that will make your day a bit easier and who knows? You might even enjoy going to school.

No surprises. We talked about how kids love stability. They need to know how you are going to respond to every situation. They need to think of you as their 'Rock.' Your kids need to have a clear understanding of what is expected of them. Always. And when they stray and they will, the way you handle yourself is just as important as what you say. Remember. Discipline is not punishment. It's people building. Most of the kids I had were not mean-spirited. They just didn't know how to be. That sounds awful, but it's true. I couldn't believe the amount of talking and how loud some of my classes were. "Jimmy, I know you're only ten years old and haven't been around that long, but how many times are you going to tell that story? Class, raise your hand if you have heard that story before." Picture 25 kids raising their hands as one. "Jimmy, why don't you live a few more years, save up some new stories, then come back. We would love to hear them. Class, raise your hand if you would like Jimmy to come back in a few years and tell us some new stories." Picture 25 kids and a teacher raising their hands as one.

"I'm standing right here," was a familiar response to some of the more excitable storytellers.

"Are you this loud when your family is driving in the car somewhere?"

"I can imagine what dinner at your house is like." Excessive talking is a big problem. If a kid is talking, he isn't listening. We did implement specific structures to combat the problem; Quiet time, Chat Time, red and green squares, Show and Tell. And those do help, but the only way to get your kids to realize that there is a better way to use the school day is to build a Family within the classroom. A Family that cares and values each member of that Family. And your kids will see those benefits when they are immersed in a self-contained elementary setting.

Parents don't like surprises either. Even if you haven't heard from them in forever, as soon as Jimmy takes his unfavorable report card home…suddenly, Mom wants to know what the hell is going on. Communicate and keep records. In this age of tech, it's easy. I always kept folders on all my kids. I wrote the dates of every note, phone call, and later on, e-mail for every parent communication. If you have developed the Teacher to Parent connection, this is not a problem. Throw in the fact that you have an open-door policy, and you are covered. If you haven't been able to find the parents with a search warrant, let your principal know what's going on. And keep that folder handy.

All kids are not the same. You can't teach them the same. You can't have the same expectations for all of them. You have to know when to push and when to pull. And most of all: you have to know when to let it go.

"Mr. Teel, how come you let Sally stand on her desk when we're cleaning the room? It's not fair." This was almost at the end of the year.

"Well, remember when she would do it every day? And yell?"

"When was the last time you saw her up there?"

"I don't know. Maybe last week."

"Was she yelling?"

"No."

"So, she's getting better. Right?"

"I guess."

"Do you want to stand on your desk?"

"I'm good."

Pick your battles, but always expect improvement. It may take a while, but when you spend all day with your kids, you really get to know them. I had another student who had trouble sitting down and being still. So I made her a deal. She loved to clean and my room was always a bit unkempt. Not dirty, mind you, but perhaps a bit unorganized. So I told her she could dust and organize my stuff as long as she could answer any question I asked her while she was cleaning. It was a win, win. She always answered correctly and my room looked good.

Although I do remember one time when she interrupted me,

"Mr. Teel, how do you live like this?" She was so good at organizing, but occasionally a stack of papers would go missing. I should have checked the closet.

If you want to see one of your kids absolutely glow, single them out in front of the class with a simple, straight from your heart, recognition of something they did. You can't do this every day, or it will lose its impact. I had a student one year who was very quiet. He didn't interact with the others. The class wasn't mean or anything. They just overlooked him. During snack time one morning, I graded the spelling tests and noticed his. Another 100. I realized that this student had not missed a single word all year. Some of the kids wanted me to yell out their grades while we ate.

"Hey, Jimmy. You got one right. Just kidding."

Then without thinking, I shouted out this particular student's score. And added, "By the way, class, he hasn't missed a single word all year." They looked stunned for a second. Then, smiles, and some 'good jobs.' I glanced at the young man. He wasn't comfortable being in the limelight. I knew that, but I just felt it needed to be said. I noticed a faint smile on his face while he finished his crackers. I swear the kids treated him just a little bit differently for the rest of the year.

I never had a nickname. Most kids don't. But it's important to some and it can be another way to build connections in your classroom. So, we had a tradition of nicknames for those who wanted one. Some were easy to come up with. I have actually come up with some on the first day of school. Others would take longer. There wasn't a process. They just evolved.

I named one of my students Goober.' I don't know why. He was kind and generous. A real nice kid.

One day out of nowhere he said, "Mr. Teel. I don't want you to call me Goober anymore."

"OK," I replied.

"Why do you call me Goober?"

"Because Goober is an old name for peanuts, and I love peanuts." Sometime after lunch, I was giving a Math lesson, and out of nowhere.

"Mr. Teel. You can call me Goober."

I used to play basketball with the kids at recess every once in a while. One of my kids was showing some pretty good moves, so I started calling him, 'Twinkle Toes.' I think he was a little embarrassed at first. I don't think he had ever heard it before. Eventually, he realized that it was a term of respect. I got a card from him when he graduated from sixth grade. He signed it, 'Twinkle Toes.'

There were times when I had trouble pronouncing names. Even easy ones. I kept calling one student the wrong name because I used a long a sound instead of a short e. After about three weeks, she reminded me again and said her name rhymes with melon.

"Oh. Like Melon Head?"

"Yes."

For the rest of the year, she signed her papers, Melon Head.

This is the strangest nickname story. One morning one of my kids came in with her head down a bit. I noticed her

hair was different. She seemed to be trying to cover her face.
"What's the matter?"

"Look."

"Oh my God!"

On her forehead just under her hairline was the largest zit I had ever seen! "Good Lord. Are we having an eclipse? You're blocking the sun. Now I know where Pluto went."

I would not have released such comments if there wasn't a connection between us. I knew she could handle it. She actually thought they were funny. Here's the teachable moment. Not just for her, but for the whole class. I told them how bad my zits were when I was in school and how I learned to cope with all of it. "Don't hide it. Come into the room and show it to the world. If you bring it up first, you have shown that it's no big deal to you."

"I'm sixty years old and I still get zits. I've had the same one for so long that I named it."

OK. You're getting ahead of me. This really sweet, kind girl decided to celebrate her zit by naming it. I'm not sure who came up with it, but she started to sign all of her papers with her name and 'Ginger.' We had fun with it all year. Sometimes I would take attendance the old way. I would call out the kids' names and wait for the 'present.' When I got to the young lady, I would call her name. 'Present.' Ginger?

'Present.'

I can't believe what a good sport she was. The next year I was walking down the hall when I saw her coming toward me. She had a big smile on her face.

"Mr. Teel, Ginger is gone!"

"That's great."

We talked a little. She said that she was doing fine and that she was happy. As I walked down the hall, I couldn't help but feel a bit sad.

I missed Ginger.

Teachers have favorites. I treated all of my kids with respect and I truly cared about each and every one. But as I explained to a student one day, teachers are people, too.

"Well, don't you have people you would rather hang out with than others?"

"So do I."

"So, who's your favorite kid in our class?"

I looked around the room, searching. Spotted the student who was reading and eating a doughnut and pointed. She signed all of her papers 'The Chosen One.' Having nicknames in your classroom may not sound like a big deal, but it's another piece. It can strengthen the connections you are building. It is another example of showing your kids that you are going deeper. You are pulling the layers of the onion off and genuinely getting to know your kids.

Kids will respond. Some kids will naturally make a connection with you. But most will wait for the teacher. It's our job as the teacher to get them to buy what we are selling. It's our job to initiate the connection. That Student to Teacher baseline of the Triangle. The trust you build in your classroom is the most effective teaching tool you will ever have.

We all know that every year is different. Some classes just take longer to gel, and you won't be able to grab them all. But if the next grade level is also a self-contained environment, you have a much better chance. Just imagine the cumulative effect on our kids if they are immersed in this stable, safe, and purposeful learning community for six years.

And if you Loop. Oh my God! Watch them soar.

Chapter Twenty: I Need a Fix

I wrote this little primer to show Elementary teachers that teaching in a self-contained classroom will lead to Daily Rewards. Not the kind of rewards you get for shopping at Safeway, but life-changing rewards. When you take advantage of what this educational environment offers, everyone in the Student-Teacher-Parent Triangle reaps those rewards. Your students certainly do. They feel safe, they feel like they belong. And they feel that level of trust that is missing in so many of our kids' lives. It may take a while for some, but you will even see parents come around. And after this pandemic year, I'm sure they have a better understanding of what teachers go through. That wall will slowly disappear. And for you teachers who already have parental involvement, it gets even better. And in this family environment where the relationships are real, teachers become more effective, students are more receptive. Your room will be where 'Great Learning' is happening.

Whether you measure student success with EOY standardized test scores, Graduation rates, or even attendance percentages, your students will measure up. When I was in the classroom, I realized that if you focus on the short-term goals, the long-term goals will fall into place.

The stuff you do day in and day out. I wanted my kids smiling when they left and wanting to show up the next morning. If you want to see them really smile, let them dance out the door. We used to put on a song about three minutes before dismissal, crank it up, and dance out the door and down the hall. 'Happy' by Pharrell was our favorite. Loved it.

Even our middle school and high school teachers will reap the benefits of your efforts. Because you are not only sending well-prepared students on, you're sending well-prepared people.

The pandemic has had an incredible impact on this school year. The upcoming years are shrouded in uncertainty. We need to be ready. We need to learn from this year. What worked. What didn't work. We need to share with each other at every level: local, state, and national. Things were different this year. No students, some students, virtual learning, half schedules. But I'm convinced. Teaching is Teaching. Creating genuine relationships with our students and building a Family of those students is possible whether we're in person or online. We should be able to take all that we have learned and incorporate it into what we know already works.

Have you noticed that there are just times in your life where opportunities present themselves? Where doors magically open up. That one open seat in the lecture hall that leads to a wedding ceremony. Or playing centerfield on a coed softball team where the left fielder is an elementary school principal (Yes, blame him). I truly believe that this is one of those times. It just feels right. There is a light at the end of this tunnel. I am really excited. I can see the possibilities. What a wonderful time to get back in the classroom to start your Family. Build that trust, and add all the ideas that resourceful teachers across the country have created. The opportunity has presented itself. The door has opened up. The timing feels right.

It's time to build something special for these young kids. It's time to lay the foundation that we can build on each year that they are in Elementary school. We owe it to them. And as they grow, so do we.

In addition to implementing Self-Contained Elementary schools, there are a few other things we need to look at.

We need to take a good look at how we are preparing teachers. In addition to knowing what to teach, these newbies need to be prepared for what they are walking into. School districts need to provide mentoring programs. Strong, relatable mentoring programs that are actually meaningful and helpful. Programs that teach techniques and provide tools that these new teachers can use in the classroom immediately. My first school district was fantastic. I was paired with a mentor who actually guided me through my first year. She helped develop my lesson plans and offered suggestions, but mostly listened. My school provided the time for me to observe other teachers in my school. Watching how a teacher handled certain situations was invaluable.

In-services and workshops need to be well-thought-out, useful and tailored to specific needs. If I could use something I learned from a workshop in my classroom the very next day; that was a good workshop.

We need more men in elementary schools. A lot of kids are missing that role model. Kids need to be around strong men who are also kind and compassionate. I mean actual classroom teachers. I know that was my greatest asset. I was 43 when I started teaching. It did take a few years to find my way, but when I settled in, I was able to bring all of my life experiences and I would like to think a bit of wisdom to the classroom. I would like to see school districts work in conjunction with State and private agencies to provide a pipeline of sorts to get more men teachers in our Elementary schools. Retired military officers seems like a good place to start.

Parental Involvement. I know, I know. Most teachers never want to see a parent in their classroom. The neat thing about being self-contained is that both philosophies can work. We already talked about how to use parents in your class, and how you will benefit. But you can also build your Family within the classroom without any parental involvement whatsoever. You as the central figure in the room all day every day are essentially the mom or dad. It can work.

I hear people all the time say, "Well, when the pandemic is over, we can all get back to normal," I agree, for jobs, and restaurants, and hugs. But not for school. For the most part, Normal doesn't work. Especially now. So many kids are going to be behind because of the pandemic. What a perfect opportunity to get everyone on the same page. Let's make the commitment. Let's commit to Self-Contained Elementary Schools for Kinder through Fifth Grade. Let's create environments where kids feel safe and feel like they belong. A place where they understand why they are there. Let's create environments where parents feel included, and know that their kids are not only being taught but are being loved. Let's create environments where teachers can see tangible results from their efforts. A place where teaching and learning happen year after year after year. A place where teachers actually want to be. A place filled with Daily Rewards.

Let's fix this.
Let's do it for our kids and their families.
Let's do it for our teachers.
And, yes. Let's do it for Richard.

Just a thought: Every once in a while, come home after school, pour yourself a glass of wine and re-read a chapter. Or better yet. Write one of your own.

Epilogue

In Miss Crosetto's Honors English class, we were responsible for two oral book reports. One in front of the class and one in front of her. We had to make an appointment after school for hers. I remember mine quite well.

I had chosen To Kill a Mockingbird. I managed to squeeze it in with all the other stuff that goes on in High School.

I showed up on time. Sat down in the chair next to her desk. I noticed that it was positioned just like a witness chair next to the judge's bench. Miss Crosetto motioned me to sit down while she continued to work on something. I started right in with the title and the author. She barely looked up while asking me questions about the book. Concrete and abstract questions. I felt like everything was going pretty well. Then she asked me if the story ended like I thought it would.

I felt that same empty feeling in my stomach like I had when I was standing in my soaked R.O.T.C. uniform outside her locked classroom. I suddenly realized that I hadn't finished reading it. Oh my God! I am sitting next to the Matriarch of a New Jersey Mafia family! I am completely wasting her time. I just hung myself out to dry. I felt the sweat forming on my forehead. I'm sure she could see it, even without looking up.

After an awkward silence, she put her pencil down and said that she had to run to the office and make a phone call. And that it would probably take about 20 minutes.

As soon as she closed the door behind her, I grabbed the book and frantically searched for any familiar-looking page. Found it. It wasn't too bad. I scanned the part I had not finished and took a deep breath.

She calmly walked in, sat down, apologized, and repeated the same question. Miss Crosetto had two choices. She could have taken the route of most other teachers and yelled at me for not being ready, and that her time was valuable. She could have brought up responsibility, and organization. But she knew me. She chose the path that great teachers take. The path that teaches. That often referred to 'Teachable Moment.'

That book report was fifty years ago.
Teacher to Student Connection.
Student to Teacher Connection.
Lifetime Connection.

Printed in the USA
CPSIA information can be obtained
at www.ICGtesting.com
CBHW081704080224
4021CB00004BB/42